THE INE
PUZZLE®

6 Aspects of Powerful Executive Presence

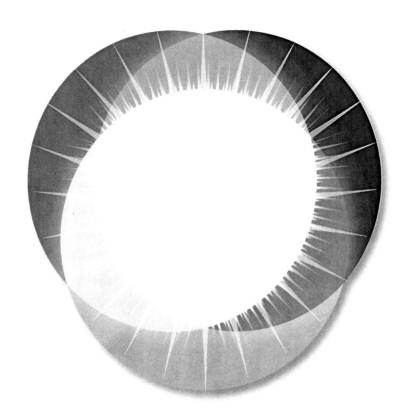

By Val Williams

The Influence Puzzle®

6 Aspects of Powerful Executive Presence

Published by Shadowbrook Publishing
P.O. Box 2458
Edison, New Jersey 08818

Library of Congress Control Number: 2008909100

ISBN 10: 0-9796371-0-4

ISBN 13: 978-0-9796371-0-0

Table of Contents

The Influence Puzzle®
is for senior executive
leaders who:

➤ See leadership more as a calling than a job.

➤ Value both success and meaning.

➤ Realize that in business, as in life:

> *Your own presence is the most*
> *strategic tool you have.*

My Purpose

Whether I am facilitating a management retreat, coaching an individual executive, speaking to an audience, writing a book, or consulting with an organization, it all comes down to the same thing for me.

The true spirit of my work is to:

➤ *Reconnect leaders at the top of the house with that powerful feeling of confidence they get when they believe in their own leadership.*

Such confidence means not depending on your executive job title, your company's clout or the well-connected people you know. The powerful feeling of confidence I am talking about comes from knowing that you are able to influence things through your presence, your own way of being. That feeling says:

"I have the power to engage people, to move people, so that together we influence how things turn out. Let's do this!"

Val Williams

1

Introduction

> *"Let him that would move the world first move himself."*
>
> *- SOCRATES*

When I started writing this book, I wanted the opening line to be something really provocative, something interesting and deep, so that you, the reader, would keep reading. I sat at my computer ready to type. I had visions of sitting on the couch at the Today Show, with Matt Lauer asking me how I came up with such a brilliant opening for my new bestseller. I really had planned on dazzling you with an exciting start.

After an hour of trying to come up with the exact right words for the book's opening line ... I had nothing so dazzling.

Then I remembered something my own coach had said to me: "Just describe the real way this book came about. Just tell your story."

So, here is my story.

Throughout my life I have enjoyed observing how things work, how they are put together. As a kid, I always liked figuring things out. In school I loved science class and learning things like how the human body functioned or how planets revolved around the sun. I was amazed the first time I watched a baby bird come out of an egg. When I played in the field across the street from my house, I used to spend hours watching insects. I was fascinated by the way caterpillars made cocoons, how spiders spun webs and how ants carried food and worked together. I liked to play games like checkers, chess and dodge ball, because you had to figure out how the game worked in order to win.

I was always drawn to understanding how things happened. I enjoyed exploring simple things in a deep way by observing, listening and asking lots of questions. And I was most delighted when I was surprised — when it turned out that things were not as they appeared. Watching the caterpillar in the cocoon looked like life was over for the caterpillar, but it wasn't! It was a change in form. Whether I was learning in school, watching grasshoppers or playing a game, the best feeling of all was that excitement of discovering: *"Oh! That's how that works. That's how the pieces of the puzzle fit together."*

Fast forward to my adult life. After being a corporate executive in the healthcare industry for several years, I started my own business in executive leadership development. Over the last 14 years I have very happily spent most of my time coaching senior executives and their teams on leadership development. Our constant question has been simple: "How can we continually get better at leading people so that we get better business results?" As expected, we have often worked together on senior-level leadership skills such as vision development, alignment, strategic planning, delegation, execution, conflict and communication.

However, the one topic that my clients and I started getting deeply interested in was their ability to influence, especially to influence people so that the business results were stronger. We started to see that even when my executive clients developed stronger leadership skills, there was still a huge opportunity for them to be more effective as leaders. *Especially at the more senior VP and C levels, we realized that coaching on leadership skills alone — even high-level, senior leadership skills such as strategy and vision development — was not enough to support them in being as successful as they wanted to be. Now that they were at the top of the organization, they wanted to do more.*

My clients were growing as leaders and they could demonstrate progress during their coaching, but they (and I) wanted to go further. They wanted to have an even more powerful impact on the business. Envisioning even larger returns on their investment of time and energy, they could see that more was possible for them as leaders. They wanted to inspire people at a deeper level, be a catalyst to enable their business to move more quickly, and influence outcomes more effectively.

My clients were overall very successful and skilled senior executives. So, what was missing? Now this was a puzzle.

Through coaching hundreds of executives over several years, I learned that the next level in my clients' leadership effectiveness and influence only came when we also worked specifically on strengthening their underlying executive presence.

As my clients and I got further into executive presence development, we realized that executive presence is a complex topic. The term has many different and wide-ranging definitions for people. Some people define executive presence as that intangible charisma you feel when someone who has it walks into a room. Some people think executive presence is oral presentation skills when a leader gives speeches. Some think executive presence has to do with clothes, grooming and body language. Some say that they have no idea what executive presence is; they just know it when they see it. Others dismiss the whole topic as too vague to really work with.

Somewhere along the way I realized that I had a personal pull toward this topic. I felt a real calling around working with executives specifically on developing the kind of executive presence I was finding so important. I was starting to realize that this particular type of executive presence was critical for successful senior executive leadership, and I wanted to develop more clarity around the idea. I felt the need to get leaders into conversations so that we could build some new definitions around what powerful executive presence really means. My burning question became: *"Who do you need to be to really impact people and results?"* It was another intriguing part of the puzzle.

Slowly it dawned on me that I was on the same journey myself. I realized that in order to help senior executives develop the kind of executive presence I had in mind, I would have to develop it in myself. I saw that my approach to presence would require me to be living my own model for presence. I knew I would not need to be perfect at it or have it completely mastered, but in order to have credibility and impact, I would have to personally be on the same path as my clients.

I started looking at my most successful senior executive clients to figure out what they had in common when it came to presence. Then I coached other clients to develop some of those qualities. Meanwhile, I was working with my own coach to develop those same qualities in myself. And it was not so easy.

I am deeply grateful to all my clients. Each of them has taught me some aspect of what eventually became my model for executive presence. In a way, my clients and I became an informal learning community, all teaching each other what outstanding leadership presence looked and felt like. Although many of my clients have not met each other, without realizing it we all helped each other grow and learn and develop strategies to get to the next level of leadership presence — the type of presence that has significant impact on people and results. We evolved each other upward. And in the process the pieces of the puzzle of "how to influence through presence" came together.

Along the way, I noticed that in today's business world, there's a lot of material out there about "executive presence", and much of it doesn't coincide with what I'm talking about. Hence my choice of a fresher term that you will see throughout the book: "influential presence."

It has definitely been an inside-out approach. As I started getting better at actually living some of these attributes,

I could better see how to write about them. In the end, through working with my clients, I learned that there are six key ingredients to a powerful presence that influences people and moves them to action. A leader who possesses this added ability to influence people naturally also automatically better influences business results. In the end, my learning and experiences throughout this journey resulted in the six- part model called The Influence Puzzle®.

Executive Summary

S ince senior executive leaders usually want the big picture and the bottom line first, here is a summary of this book.

The book walks you through three messages:

1. What's so Tough about Being a Senior Executive?

This is a summary of the exploration my clients and I did when looking at the unique challenges of being a senior executive leader (Vice President through C Level). Although it often looks like a wonderful thing to be in charge, senior leaders know that *there are some very difficult issues to manage when you are at the top in an organization. And the way you meet these challenges can be the difference between your success and failure.*

2. The Opportunity for Senior Leaders

Through individual coaching with senior executives and facilitating group seminars with their teams, I realized that our work together has always been an inquiry. We always seemed to be asking questions like: Why does senior leadership have to be this tough? What are the key factors that help a leader cut through the noise to powerfully affect people and results?

The goal of our work always has been to create opportunity for leaders and to develop customized strategies that make senior leadership more effective and easier for the leader. So this section is a summary of what is possible for senior leaders. My clients and I have realized that *there is a huge opportunity for leaders to be more effective at influencing things.* That opportunity lies in leaders learning how to leverage their own influential presence as a foundation for solutions.

3. Solutions for Leaders

Based on the challenges senior leaders face and our inquiry into what drives those challenges, this section is a solution, a tool for leaders: *The Influence Puzzle®. The Influence Puzzle® is a six-part model for actively developing your own presence as a powerful leader.* The pieces of the puzzle are The 3 Ps: Purpose, Power and Peace; and The 3 Cs: Clarity, Courage and Connection. For each of the six parts, you will see a broad definition of that part, what it looks like and feels like, and examples of clients (anonymous to protect confidentiality) using or misusing that quality.

In this section I also give examples of my own personal journey to developing the six aspects of influential presence, so you will see my struggle to live The Influence Puzzle®. And of course, I am still working on living the model today. Although the model has a framework, there are no rigid rules for living it. The Influence Puzzle® gives a leader plenty of room to be authentic— to be who you really are, only more effective.

In short, this is my message:

> We have a huge opportunity to increase our positive impact as leaders.

> Leadership, especially at the top of organizations, is largely about one thing: Influence. Real influence comes from something deeper than skills and techniques. The key to the puzzle of influence is the leader's presence. That key is based solely on you. *The power of your influence is the power of your presence.*

> In today's environment of information overload, unless there is an emotionally compelling reason for people to listen to you, they don't. *It is your presence, not your authority, that creates that compelling reason.*

> Executive presence is not vague. Although presence is, in some ways, a puzzle, it can be well defined and actively developed. Based on what I have learned

from working with successful senior executives, I am suggesting six pieces for solving the puzzle. These pieces are ways of being that you and I can develop in ourselves to build a powerful presence that is the key to influence.

➤ Here's what I care about most: With this powerful, influential presence, the impact we can have as leaders could change the world.

Why Is It Important for Senior Executives to Focus on The Influence Puzzle?

Influence *n.* the power to indirectly or intangibly impact a person, group or event; power to cause a change in the character, thought or action of a person or group

Puzzle *n.* a question or problem designed for testing ingenuity; a problem or situation difficult to solve; mentally challenging

Ingenuity *n.* inventive imagination or skill; clever design or construction; skill in devising or combining

Key *n.* a means of gaining or preventing entrance, possession, or control; an instrumental or deciding factor; something that gives an explanation or provides a solution

A **puzzle** is a game or problem that challenges our ingenuity, skill or intelligence. A puzzle requires us to piece things together in such a way that we get the desired shape, picture or solution. A puzzle can be a form of entertainment and/or a problem situation that causes doubt and indecision. Either way, in order to successfully solve a puzzle, it takes creativity, multiple ways of looking at things and recognition of underlying factors.

You may feel that you are already a successful leader, and that you actually do have a strong influential presence. So why focus on the puzzle of how we influence? Why work on your presence, which is the key to The Influence Puzzle®?

Because a leader's presence is the most strategic tool they have, the most successful leaders continually and consciously strengthen the quality of their presence. This is very similar to successful companies. They have a strong brand, a strong strategy and clear vision; yet they constantly work to live these qualities fully in the marketplace and to update themselves quickly as the market changes.

How the World Has Changed

For you as a senior executive leader, there is a greater need today than in the past for strong influential presence. Business changes more frequently now. There are more mergers, acquisitions and internal reorganizations. Look at the fast pace of business, rapid technology changes, the virtual impact of geographically dispersed teams, matrixed management and reporting structures, the difficulty of retaining people. *Any one of these factors can make the strategies you use for leading today obsolete tomorrow.* Therefore, you must constantly influence people inside and outside your organization, showing them the value that you and your team bring. Otherwise, we see how easily and quickly people and functions are eliminated.

All leaders are vulnerable in this competitive market. But when your presence is not being felt, you are much more vulnerable. Without a presence that has a powerful impact on people and results and connects with your various audiences, your long-term survival is questionable. And it is easy for your presence not to be felt. In today's business world where multi-tasking and overwhelm rules, it is increasingly difficult to simply get another person's attention. *Unless there is an emotionally compelling reason for people to listen to you, they don't. It is your presence, not your authority, that creates that compelling reason.*

As a leader today, the talent pool of the people you lead has also changed. Retaining the best talent on your team is more challenging now. Talented people can relocate easily and they can work anywhere, particularly in the current virtual work environment. This current generation of workers is not at all like the Baby Boomers of the past. This generation has far greater technology and many more choices. This generation is motivated differently and often has a different set of values. Your presence as a leader — who you are — means more to them. They were not trained in the "command and control" styles of the past.

Influence and presence have always been important components of effective leadership. But the current rate of change in the world necessitates leaders who consciously sharpen the power of their presence. Leaders also need a strategy for continually strengthening their presence as the world continues to change.

Is Executive Development Real Work?

Many leaders see their own executive leadership development as something they'll get to if they have time after they do what they consider the "real work." But in my experience with senior executives, if you are not continually developing yourself, your work consists of fighting today's fires instead of finding solutions for tomorrow's growth. (And at the senior level, which one gets rewarded?)

As a senior executive, you may worry that working on yourself will take time away from the important things you have to do. However, given the level of responsibility you hold, the most important work you can do is to increase your capacity to think clearly and respond most effectively.

In terms of timing, when should a leader work on executive development? Some leaders see their professional development as that obligatory action plan that they write after their annual performance evaluation. *But actually, executive leadership development needs to be worked on every day. In fact, if you are not developing yourself every day as a leader, you are falling behind.*

Unlike in the past, business moves and changes too fast today for a leader to use the same techniques and strategies they used yesterday. So the idea that you can review your development a few times a year is risky, if not naive. Your development must be part of your daily to-do list.

How Deep Does Executive Development Have to Go?

Think of when you first became a manager. At the early levels of leadership, much of your leadership development was probably aimed at strengthening skills: how to manage people and projects, create plans, monitor resources. As with all leaders, you needed these basic skills and so this development was useful.

At the point that an executive moves into senior executive leadership, however, the focus for development clearly shifts from tactical to strategic. Skill development does continue, but the skills are higher-level, such as vision/ mission creation, team alignment, strategic planning and execution, and succession planning. Again, such upper-level skill development for senior executives is critically important for success. (For more on these executive skills, see the book *Executive Foundation* by Val Williams and Ellen Fredericks.)

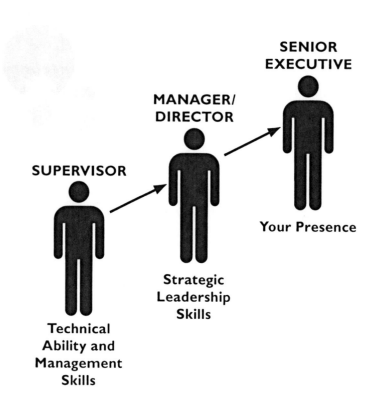

SENIOR EXECUTIVE

MANAGER/ DIRECTOR

SUPERVISOR

Your Presence

Strategic Leadership Skills

Technical Ability and Management Skills

However, even when given tools, training, and executive coaching on these higher level leadership skills, many executives are still not as effective as they'd like to be. They definitely improve in many areas, but either the improvement is not enough or it is not consistent and sustainable over time. In working with my own clients, I discovered that the most successful gains came when we worked at a much deeper level than skill development and leadership competencies alone. *Our greatest success came when we combined traditional executive development work with a serious exploration of how the leader's personal presence drives results.*

It became clear that at the most senior levels in organizations, although a leader has authority, authority is not what drives results. Successful senior leaders know that talented, inspired people drive results. The key to leadership at the senior executive levels is being able to influence those talented people. Influence is not about just skills — even high-level leadership skills like strategy and planning and vision development. All those skills help to create an excellent base. But *influence* is about *who a leader is*. The real key to influence is your presence.

Many people may think that senior executive development does not have to go very deep. Often, senior executives themselves feel that they only need to sharpen their ability to focus on producing better business results. They are usually willing to do some basic self-assessments as part of that, but sometimes that's about it. Truly successful executive leaders, however, go much further into self-exploration than is traditionally suggested. Those leaders also realize that business in the future will require more of executive leaders than in the past.

The way we even look at senior executive development may be inadequate for the way business is evolving and changing. Executive development must go deeper. The game of leadership at the top of the house has gotten tougher. The power of a leader's influence will be an even more significant factor in their success. And a leader's presence is what determines that influence.

Readiness for Development of Influence Based on Presence

Readiness *n.* the state of being prepared or available for action; willing; prompt in understanding

Although I feel strongly that the development of influential presence is the key to a senior executive leader's effectiveness, a leader has to be ready for this work. If the process is to be effective, there is a readiness factor that must be assessed before a leader dives into developing his or her presence. This is similar to the concept of business readiness, where a company does a readiness assessment as part of a merger or acquisition process. Even if you have a great idea, not everyone is ready to engage in it.

So, in order to really benefit from this book and this work, I will ask you to go deeper than usual and take a sincere, unblinking look at who you are as a person. In executive coaching work with individual executives, and in seminars with leadership teams, I have noted that the leaders who make the biggest gains are those who are ready to do this work for their own reasons. For them it goes beyond the fact that their company thought it was a good idea, or their coach recommended they focus on executive presence. Readiness comes from the leader's personal wish to seriously accelerate his or her growth as a leader and as a person.

Readiness also means that the leader has the tenacity to continue, even when the self-exploration gets uncomfortable. *Readiness means the leader understands the distinction between "relief" and "freedom."* For example, an executive can come to coaching because he or she is struggling with a particular event or challenge. Through good coaching and the executive's commitment, their performance starts to improve. Things at work are better. They experience "relief" from whatever prompted them to work on themselves. But then they quit prematurely. They have not actually completed the work necessary for real "freedom" from the root causes of their struggle, but they feel better, they're relieved. In genuine readiness, the leader goes for the full result of freedom.

So, as much as I would like to work with every senior executive on strengthening their influential presence, not every executive is ready or interested or a match for the offer. *The Influence Puzzle® is an invitation for senior executive leaders who are willing to take on a new way of being.*

The Influence Puzzle®

Now let's take a look at The Influence Puzzle® in three sections:

➤ First we will look at the unique challenges of senior executive leadership and what leaders are struggling with in "**What's So Tough About Being a Senior Executive?**"

➤ Then we will look at the opportunity for leaders to be more effective through shifting their perspective in "**The Opportunity for Senior Leaders.**"

➤ Finally, in "**A Solution for Leaders,**" we will walk through the six-part Influence Puzzle Model— a blueprint for senior executive leaders who want to build their executive presence and be more influential.

4

What's So Tough About Being a Senior Executive?

Tough *adj.* **demanding, difficult; strong enough to withstand great strain without tearing or breaking.**

One of the first steps in understanding the puzzle of how to have influence as a senior executive leader is looking at the job itself. The job is difficult. What's so tough about being a senior executive? There are several answers to the question. For starters: the workload, the people and the inevitable self-doubt.

The Workload

If you are a senior executive, although job titles vary across companies (Vice President, C-level Executive, Director), it means that you are one of the people leading a major business unit, a strategic function in the company, or the overall direction of the organization. To be a senior executive means that what you do matters to the company's bottom line in a real and significant way.

You have worked hard to get where you are. You have been smart and persistent and adaptive. You made it up the ladder to the senior executive ranks. Now that you have arrived there, some people think you must have it made. Many people wish they could be in your shoes: the one in charge, the senior leader. So what can be so tough about it now that you are on top? Haven't you achieved your dream?

It is true that being a senior executive leader in a corporation is often exciting, rewarding, and an excellent way to learn. It has many perks. And then there is the flip side: To say that corporate life is a "challenge" is an understatement!

As a senior executive you may be feeling overwhelmed with the amount of work on your plate and the pressure you feel to respond quickly to a huge number of demands: endless email, voicemail, unanticipated changes on deliverables, unplanned meeting requests, travel. In spite of the long hours you work and your multi-tasking, you may still quietly fear that you can't keep up with the fast pace. And the pace is relentless!

Here you are, facing more complex business problems than ever before, and yet you don't ever get enough time to really think about long-term strategic solutions. Urgency and firefighting seem to be the norm, so you may have learned to live with a constant, low-grade feeling of anxiety in the back of your mind all the time.

The People

And then there are the people issues. ***Even if you think of yourself as a good leader, you may be noticing that you don't have as much influence as you would like.*** You may see a variety of subtle signs, such as the ones that my executive clients and I have noticed:

➤ Feeling impatient that you have to push hard to get people's attention and can't consistently get people to do what you need them to do.

➤ Having to follow up repeatedly to get deliverables from people. You may find yourself irritated and wondering, "Why don't people just do their job?"

➤ Feeling that you keep your staff updated on things, but noticing there's not really a "team" feeling.

➤ People don't seem to be inspired to come up with innovative ideas.

➤ When you lead cross-functional project teams, it may take a lot of strong-talking and arm-waving to get people moving.

➤ Even if you have good presentation skills, you may not be sure that people really get it; it's unclear if they are buying in to your vision.

➤ Every day you face the annoyance of trying to impact difficult people who do not report to you.

➤ Somehow, although you sense the direction the company needs to take and you try to get co-workers to join in a new creative way of working, people are not really responding. You may feel concerned that the company is missing some important strategic opportunities.

➤ Feeling annoyed that peers seem to do things without considering the impact on your area. Even though you are part of a senior leadership team, you might feel disappointed that the senior team is not really working together; individual agendas and silos still get in the way of true collaboration.

➤ Noticing that you and your team are not influencing the big picture of the company's growth and momentum as much as you would like.

If any of these signs resonate with you, or if you've thought of others, chances are good that you and your company would benefit if you had greater influence.

The Self-doubt

For many senior executives, even those who are rated highly and performing well, the pressure of being at the top invites self-doubt. In addition, there are usually other people who are happy to second-guess and criticize your views and decisions. And we won't even talk about the endless politics that most senior executives have to navigate.

So sometimes, at the end of your overworked, 12- to 14-hour day...as you do the now-automatic check of your BlackBerry...you notice that you would have liked to have spent more time with your family, friends or your exercise plan that day. And after thinking briefly about all the difficulties of the day, on top of everything else, you privately question your own contribution. You are struggling to have an impact and you start wondering: *"Am I making the best use of my time? Am I doing the right things? Am I as smart as I thought I was? How come I am in charge, but I'm not sure if I'm making a real difference?"*

And you realize that if this internal questioning, this self-doubt, does not get addressed, you can start to play defensively, make safer and more conservative choices, take fewer risks, and then business results will take a hit.

Finally, in addition to the very normal self-doubt that develops when you are not sure you are influencing things enough (that self-doubt must, of course, be hidden at all costs!), there is also the pressure of survival. There is the very real possibility that you could be passed over for promotion, fired, or re-organized out of a job at any moment, even if your performance is good.

At the senior levels, there is no real job security. Many variables impact who gets in, or who stays in, a particular job; and the variables are tough to predict. *There is built-in insecurity in the senior ranks.* You may feel that your success is dependent upon holding on to this executive job position, but you realize that you may not be able to control that.

In summary: What's so tough about being a senior corporate executive? A lot!

Based on my own experience as a corporate executive and many years of coaching other senior executives in a variety of industries and locations, I can say that whether a leader voices it or not, there are some days that being a senior executive leader is just painful.

NO, Successful Leaders Do Not Suffer!

Suffer *v.* **to experience, feel or endure pain or distress; to sustain loss or harm**

Many executives are high achievers. High achievers are all about successfully reaching goals and continually moving up to take on bigger goals. *High achievers do not like to admit that they are struggling. They certainly don't want to admit when they are actually suffering.* I was advised when writing this book not to even use words like "suffering" or "pain" because it would sound too negative to senior executives. High-potential people don't even want to hear words like that. I was told to stay on the bright side and just fast-forward to the solution.

But what I have seen in the real world of leadership is that a great many senior executive, high-achieving leaders do suffer at times. Even the best leaders sometimes have days when they are experiencing something uncomfortable that lasts longer than they want, that they did not choose and that they cannot control. Having to hide your discomfort not only creates additional pressure from within but also means that people are likely to minimize the difficulties you are facing.

So why is it important to acknowledge the struggle?

Because when we hide our difficulty, we usually are not

focused on doing something about it. ***Even when you are very smart and very talented, it is easy to lose your way in an organization.*** For most executives, the organization is a complex system with many moving parts, fast changes, and lots of people, emotions and politics. It's natural as a leader to try to look as if you have it all together. But trying to live inside a perfect leadership image brings its own problems. This is especially true for the more successful leaders. When I was an executive (and a high achiever), my high-achiever friends and I used to say, "When you look really good, you don't get any help." Back then, we struggled along in silence.

Bottom line: Acknowlede the tough part of being a senior executive. Once you realize that much of the challenge and difficulty is built into the job, you can be less reactive to the difficulty. Then you can use your energy to focus on understanding the nature of the game and how to accelerate your leadership development as an influential leader.

The Opportunity for Senior Leaders

Opportunity *n.* **a favorable or promising combination of circumstances; a chance for advancement or improvement**

Although things are often tough for executive leaders, there is plenty of hope. The opportunity for leaders to increase their effectiveness is based on fully realizing a few key perspectives:

➤ Successful senior executive leadership is a head game.

➤ Senior executive leadership is about *influence* versus authority.

➤ Company leadership skill and competency lists are not enough.

➤ Real influence is based on a leader's *presence.*

The Nature of the Game:
"It's a Head Game"

Many executives do not realize that a huge part of the stress at senior leadership levels is about the nature of the corporation at that level, not just a reflection of their individual ability and talent. *Paradoxically, when leaders reach more senior levels, things change so much that they often start doubting their own ability in ways they never have before.* As one of my own coaches says, we all hit a point where we reach the end of our winning formula. The things that we used to do that made us successful no longer work.

If this describes your situation, you may think you have peaked, or that maybe you are not as good as you thought.

This is incorrect.

You are still that talented high achiever. However, you may be missing new strategies to effectively navigate the unique difficulties of senior-level leadership. Some very interesting things happen when you move from Director level through Vice President level to C level. My clients and I have noticed several shifts at higher levels of organizations:

Senior Level Leadership Demands

↑	strategic thinking	↓	time to think
↑	collaboration.	↓	relationship
↑	stress	↓	feedback/support
↑	authority	↓	need for authority
↑	compensation	↓	leisure

➤ You are being asked to be more strategic as you move higher. There is increased demand for you to be more of a thought leader, but you have decreased time to think.

➤ You have an increased need to collaborate and build alliances with your peers, but you are so busy and moving so fast that you have decreased opportunity to actually foster relationships.

➤ You have increased stress due to the complexity of your role and the intense pace, but at the higher levels you usually get decreased support in the form of feedback and coaching.

➤ You have increased authority on the organizational chart, but at the higher levels there is a decreased need for authority. Now what you need is the ability to influence without authority being a factor.

➤ You have a better compensation plan so that you can have increased quality of life with family and friends; but you have decreased time and energy for leisure activities and vacations.

These are the types of shifts that can cause you to feel less confident and experience some of the self-doubt described earlier. The way out is to realize that, in many ways, senior leadership is a head game. You have to keep your own head in the right place: remember who you are, what the game is and how to avoid the pitfalls that are just part of the game. *This means remembering to have confidence in yourself, in your own presence, your own way of being, as your primary source of power.* This is a key part of the puzzle.

The head game means that you can't let other people push your buttons. It means not taking things personally. The head game means preparing yourself to withstand criticism. It means acknowledging your limitations, but not choking under pressure. Having your head in the right place means that you realize how competitive a game it is at the senior executive level. You prepare yourself for the nature of the game: You know you are going to have some very exciting and cool experiences. And you will also have some very not cool experiences. Not everyone will like you. Not everyone will see your vision of what's possible—and that's fine. After all, the work of senior leadership is to sell your vision.

Part of the head game of senior executive leadership is knowing that some people will try to undermine you. Especially if you are very talented, you may threaten other people and they can become envious or resentful. This is not great, but it is fairly normal human behavior. So don't overreact to people who overreact to you.

The head game is not to let them throw you off balance. As I often say to executives, *"Don't be distracted by reacting to just anything someone else throws at you. If you do, you are being like a dog that chases a Frisbee.* At first, the dog runs after the Frisbee every time he sees you throw it. But after a while you can just jerk your hand with no Frisbee in it and the dog will run to chase it anyway. Don't chase Frisbees!"

Understanding the head game opens the door to the big opportunity of keeping and continually building your confidence in your own leadership. So one of the first levels of hope for a better executive leadership life is actually seeing how the game is played at the senior executive level.

The Corporation Cannot Love You Back

Why do leaders need a reminder to base their confidence on themselves and their presence versus basing their confidence on anything else? Because the organization encourages you to have confidence in things other than yourself and your own presence. Corporations reward certain behaviors. It is sometimes subtle, but usually the behaviors that are rewarded are connected with having confidence in the corporate vision, your corporate job and authority, the corporate strategy or the organization's mission, goals and values. Senior executives, in particular, are encouraged to have confidence in the corporation's history, in the company's market performance, in their company job title, and in the corporation's highest leaders.

This does not make corporations "bad", it is just how corporations function. A key goal of most corporations is long-term viability. They must create sustainable business and operations regardless of people or personalities. All these things are part of the picture at the higher levels.

However, when you put more confidence in these organizational trappings than in your own ability to be with people in a way that moves them (i.e., your presence), then you end up mistakenly thinking that you have to work harder, talk louder and do more to be successful.

31

It is not necessarily part of the corporation's role to encourage you to have, build and maintain confidence in your own presence. This is not a problem, unless you forget that building and maintaining your presence is something that you have to do for yourself every day. In spending so much of our time and energy at work, it is easy to forget that job scope and compensation do not define self-worth, even if you are a C-level success.

Again, not only does it not make corporations bad, in fact, when you see the big picture, the corporate arrangement is a very clear deal. You as a senior leader perform certain functions, and the corporation gives you a certain compensation. This is actually the total deal. A lot of the other stuff that executives project onto a corporation is, in fact, not part of the core deal. So having any of the other expectations is not really in your best interest (i.e., expectations such as looking to one's career to provide validation of self-worth, approval or a way of proving oneself). So, again, it's easy to lose your way in the corporate forest.

This is a very subtle dynamic at the senior levels of leadership. In fact, many leaders may say; "Of course, I already know this. I know the corporation can't take care of me ... I know I have to take care of myself." However, what I have seen in my work with senior executives is that *a large part of many leaders' stress is caused by expecting a level of validation and approval from the corporation (bosses, peers, etc.) that actually is never going to be available.* Many leaders think they are beyond the need for approval, but when we look at their behavior, sometimes their actions say otherwise. It is important to remember that as much as you may love the perks and the challenge and excitement of being a corporate executive ... *the corporation cannot love you back.*

In summary, one of the most important shifts in perspective is realizing the nature of the senior executive leadership game and playing accordingly.

Executive Leadership Is All About Influence vs. Authority

Influence *n.* **the power to indirectly or intangibly impact a person, group or event; power to cause a change in the character, thought or action of a person or group**

Authority *n.* **the right and power to command, enforce laws, and exact obedience**

People often think that once you become a senior executive, once you get to the higher positions in an organization, you have authority and therefore control. They may not see the big difference between having authority (which is given to you by your company) and having influence (which comes from within). However, leadership at the senior executive levels is all about the ability to influence rather than depend on authority. *And if you want to have influence, you have to develop your presence.*

Being influential means having the power to impact people and events. Being influential means that your leadership itself is able to cause a change in how people think and act. Being influential means that results are different because of you. And in order to have that type of powerful impact on people and results, you will need more than a few tips on influence skills. You'll need more than mechanical behaviors that are meant to influence. To have an impact that really influences people, you will need to have a powerful personal presence.

Presence *n.* the state of being present; a person's bearing or carriage

Presence is your way of carrying yourself, your way of being. If you are influential, your presence is something people feel when you walk in the room. The type of presence that influences people is that "it factor" that people experience with you. It's the kind of presence that moves people. If you want people to change and perform at higher levels, then they will have to feel inspired, not just be told that it's their job. *Presence is not simply about saying and doing the right things. Presence is about what people sense is behind what you say and do.*

The good news is that your presence is something you can control. It is solely based on you.

Why Company Leadership Competency Lists Are Not Enough

You might think that working on specific leadership skills or your company having a leadership competency list is enough. But as outlined earlier, *executive leadership development has to go much deeper than skills and competencies.* Even in companies where good leadership competency models exist, leaders are often not actually behaving in ways that match the company's model competency list. All the leadership practical skills you have been taught are great. They are needed. But successful leadership is about the capacity to influence through presence. Obviously, it takes some level of presence to even become an executive. *However, what is missing is a practical path, or even a conversation, about how executives can develop that underlying presence further*— into the type of presence that moves people to go beyond their comfort zone. Most leaders have not been given specific strategies for developing their personal presence.

In fact, there are very few opportunities for leaders to have meaningful discussion about the power of executive presence and how exactly to develop it.

This lack of tools for development of presence is a significant concern. At the senior executive levels, presence is no longer just a great thing to have, as it may have been at lower levels. In order to be an effective senior leader, powerful presence is essential. At the higher levels, your whole job is leadership of people. The personal presence that you radiate has a huge impact on whether or not people choose to follow you. When you demonstrate a confident and inspiring presence and people do follow you, business results are stronger. At lower levels, this presence is also nice to have, but it is less essential. And frankly, looking confident is easier to fake at the lower levels. At the senior levels, strong presence needs to be the real thing; an authentic, genuine way of being.

You need different tools for success as you continue to move to the top of the organization. *A company leadership competency list is a good beginning— a good baseline— but it is not enough for successful leadership at the senior executive levels.* For real success as a leader, you need a presence that allows you to powerfully influence people. And you need to know how to continually strengthen and develop your presence as you encounter new challenges.

Presence Goes Deeper than Presentation Skills and Body Language

Many people, even experienced leaders, think that executive presence is something you have to be born with— either you have it or you don't. Executive presence is often viewed as a vague quality that is difficult to describe and even more difficult to actually strengthen. However, I have seen that presence development is not vague and if you focus on a few specific areas, your presence can become much more powerful. The puzzle does have a solution.

Often, when leaders are trying to build their executive presence, they think of taking training classes in oral presentation skills so they can work on taking command of the room by improving their language and voice quality. Or if they are working individually with an executive coach, they assume they need to do video training to shift their body language, improve their hand gestures, posture and even dress and grooming. This type of presentation training can be useful for leaders. However, although leaders usually do see an improvement in their presentations with this tool, this type of training alone often does not build the type of powerful executive presence that a leader needs for broader, executive-level influence. Genuine, powerful, personal presence goes much deeper than good presentation and body language. *In fact, what can be seen in a leader's body on video or heard in voice tone is only the byproduct, the reflection of the leader's internal perspective.*

Real presence starts from how you as a leader view yourself and your capability. Your presence is what people experience when they are with you, and that presence is radiating from what is inside you. Presence is born in your self-perception: how you see your value to the world, how you see your power, how you see others. Your external behavior is a reflection of this perspective. How you show up is based on those internal stories you have about yourself and how you connect with others.

So, to work only at the level of presentation skill can actually be a more difficult and less effective way for a leader to try to develop. Although you can learn to control some of your body language and you can remind yourself of cues for word choice and communication skills, this can take a lot of energy if the internal work has not been done. What I have seen in my work with executive leaders is that if we work on the leader's internal perspective about who they are and their ability to influence, then much of their external behavior shifts effortlessly.

Benefits of Powerful Presence

When you strengthen your presence, when you are clear that your own presence is what makes a difference, then you radiate the type of leadership that moves people at a very deep level. With this type of presence you can engage people, inspire people to join your vision, and make some really big things happen.

The solution to many of the challenges of senior executive leadership is to have powerful and influential presence. What does that look like?

➤ When you develop this kind of presence, your daily life improves. Although you still have all the realities of the high work volume and urgent demands, you respond more intentionally and don't easily overreact.

➤ When you feel confident in your presence, then you are able to step back to see solutions to complex business problems; you are more secure in identifying the best use of your time.

➤ When you develop your presence to this degree, you take conflict in stride; you deal with challenging people more calmly, and you take the time you need to make thoughtful decisions.

➤ The more consciously you work on your presence, the more people around you seem to change. More seems to happen when you are saying less.

➤ People seek your opinion more frequently. It's easier to get and keep people's attention, so you don't have to repeat yourself as much. People are attracted to you and your vision. Getting buy-in is easier and people want to add their own creative ideas.

➤ With strong presence, you paint the big picture for teams and show people what they have in common and what can be gained by working together. You encourage people to see the connection between today's actions and tomorrow's growth for the company, and how it will benefit them—*and your people get it.*

➤ When your presence is developed to this level, people feel your arrival at the meeting and welcome your input. You are viewed as helpful and beneficial to the process, and that makes people want to follow you.

➤ *When you believe that your presence is what insures your long-term success, with or without the company, then your experience changes.* Confidence in your presence and your ability to influence protects you from damaging self-doubts. You realize the nature of the game you are playing at the senior level. Although you continually work on your development, you know when you have done your best and you can let that be enough. With confidence in your presence you no longer look to the corporation for approval and validation. You appreciate recognition for a job well done, but you are clear on your own strengths and on the value of your contribution.

➤ Instead of struggling to get people on board with you, you feel confident in your ability to impact people. You feel the excitement and energy of being able to engage people. You have that great feeling of working together with people to shape the way things turn out. You can see yourself easily leading people, encouraging them to get involved. It's as if your presence is saying to people, with enthusiasm, "Let's do this!"

A Solution for Senior Executive Leaders

Executive presence has long been shrouded in mystery. People often have difficulty clearly defining what presence is, but they know it when they see it. However, while presence appears to be a puzzle, it is actually not so vague and it can be actively developed.

The Influence Puzzle® Model helps senior executive leaders strengthen their own powerful presence. As leaders move through the six parts of the model, they can develop the type of presence that powerfully influences people and results.

The first three parts of The Influence Puzzle® Model focus on how leaders develop themselves _internally_ and create a basis for the intention of their actions. These are:

The 3 Ps
PURPOSE
POWER
PEACE

The second three parts of The Influence Puzzle® Model help a leader shape his or her *external* behavior. These are:

The 3 Cs
CLARITY
COURAGE
CONNECTION

Together, the six parts of The Influence Puzzle® Model give leaders a simple, clear blueprint for developing their own unique and powerful influential presence.

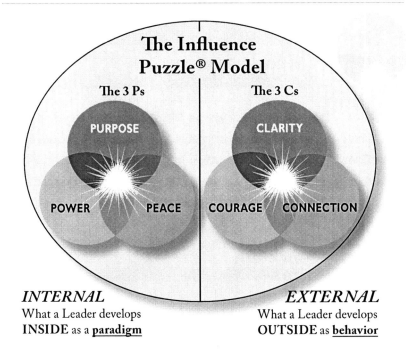

INTERNAL
What a Leader develops
INSIDE as a **paradigm**

EXTERNAL
What a Leader develops
OUTSIDE as **behavior**

Influence *n.* the power to indirectly or intangibly impact a person, group or event; power to cause a change in the character, thought or action of a person or group

Puzzle *n.* a question or problem designed for testing ingenuity; a problem or situation difficult to solve, mentally challenging

Presence *n.* the state of being present; a person's bearing or carriage

> The Influence Puzzle® Model is a tool for transforming your leadership effectiveness. It is a tool to help you strengthen your personal executive presence so that you more powerfully influence people and results.

How to Work with The Influence Puzzle® Model

There are a number of ways to work with and apply The Influence Puzzle® Model to your daily work life, including self-assessment, live application and training, a process for learning, and as a tool for ongoing executive development. Choose which approach(es) work best for you.

Self-Assessment

To have a full picture of what each way of being really looks and feels like, start by reading all six parts of The Influence Puzzle®. As you read, ask yourself how well you demonstrate that specific way of being in your own leadership. Assessment questions at the end of each section will help with this process.

Figure out which aspects you have already developed well and which aspects need more work in order for you to have a stronger presence that influences people and results. Target your reading and practice to the areas that you want to strengthen.

Live Application and Training

Some leaders work through The Influence Puzzle® Model alone. However, results are usually greater when leaders work with an Executive Coach or attend live training seminars. The Influence Puzzle® Model addresses a person's overall way of being as opposed to just behavioral tips. This transformation goes a lot deeper than skill training. *The Influence Puzzle® is a guide for a transformational experience that goes beyond just an intellectual exercise.* It is very helpful to have guidance and support as you build these new perspectives and new ways of being.

It is not that you "can't" do it on your own. It's the same thing I say about executive coaching in general: *"The coaching does two things: It gets you there faster and with less pain."*

Look for an Executive Coach who has been specifically trained to coach leaders on The Influence Puzzle® Model. These Executive Coaches have the advantage that they are personally living the model themselves, customized to their own style and who they are. Having lived it, they coach others from a place of deeply understanding what it takes to create powerful influential presence. (See the "Resources" section at the end of the book.) Also look for any of our live Influence Puzzle Seminars, which are presented for small groups of executives on site or with virtual technology.

Process for Learning

For a deep learning process, take some focused time with each of the six sections of The Influence Puzzle® Model. For example, you could choose one theme per week or month and focus on seeing how well you are manifesting that quality in you and around you before moving on to the next theme. *The Influence Puzzle® is an integrated system by which all the pieces of the puzzle need to work together for the most powerful impact.* As you work the model, look for examples of situations to share with your coach or fellow participants in which each of the six ways of being overlap and strengthen each other. Look for examples of the **sweet spots where all six aspects of The Influence Puzzle® play out simultaneously.** You will know this is happening when you discover that you are producing outstanding results through the influence of your powerful presence.

Tool for Ongoing
Executive Development

The Influence Puzzle® is not a puzzle that is solved just once. In fact, for successful leadership, this puzzle has to be solved every day. *For senior executive leaders, the puzzle of how to influence people and results is a question that arises repeatedly.* The puzzle keeps changing because it is made up of an ever-moving set of variables: business keeps changing, the world changes, the people you need to influence change, the deliverables change, and you yourself are always changing.

The senior executive's challenge is to fit all these changing, moving parts together in such a way that you have the impact that you intend. The Influence Puzzle® Model has structure to help the leader create solutions, as well as flexibility to apply to countless leadership situations. The Influence Puzzle® is three-dimensional. The puzzle of influence is similar to the Rubik's Cube: it is complex and can seem overwhelming. But when you understand the underlying principles of how it actually works, the puzzle can be successfully solved. And over time, with practice, it is solved more quickly.

The 3 Ps of Leadership

PURPOSE *n.* a result or effect that is intended or desired; the goal toward which one strives or for which one exists

> "Your time is limited, so don't waste it living someone else's life. Don't be trapped by dogma— which is living with the results of other people's thinking. Have the courage to follow your heart and intuition. They somehow know what you truly want to become. Everything else is secondary."

> – STEVE JOBS

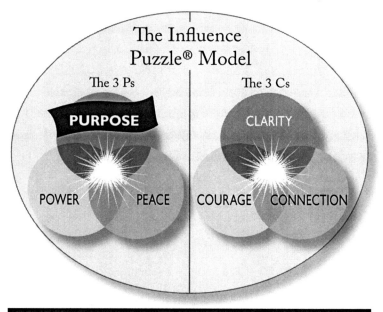

The Influence
Puzzle® Model

The 3 Ps   The 3 Cs

PURPOSE   CLARITY

POWER   PEACE   COURAGE   CONNECTION

PURPOSE

Declare the Purpose that prompted you to step up to lead.

What is Your Purpose?

Why did you choose to become a leader? Purpose is where everything starts, especially if you are a senior leader. Purpose is your answer to the question: What do you really want to accomplish? What do you deeply care about? Your purpose is reflected in your own list of personal values. Your purpose has also been referred to as your guiding principles, your key criteria for life. Think about why you became a leader: *What ultimate result did you value so much that it is the reason you stepped up to lead?* What result do you still care about so much that it motivates you to stick with the difficulty of senior leadership? That is your purpose, the reason you are in the game. And each leader's purpose is unique.

Leaders often think that purpose is only about the company. When they think of purpose, they think of the company's purpose, the company's vision and the company's mission. You are wise to be concerned about organizational vision, since it is an essential part of senior leadership. But actually, *you should be more concerned about your personal purpose.* Leaders who are clear about their own purpose, can articulate why they choose to be a leader and what they contribute are more powerful and more influential. These leaders have explored who they are as people and their credibility and confidence shines from within.

Clear Purpose: Robert

Robert is an Executive Vice President of a major snack foods company, reporting directly to the CEO. Robert has been in senior leadership positions in different companies in multiple industries.

Although his experience is varied, Robert is very clear about his purpose. I asked him once what he saw as the connection among his many successful work experiences. He said: "My number one purpose is to build leaders." No matter what job or situation he is in, Robert is there to build leaders. He believes that if he builds his peoples' leadership effectiveness, their natural talent and skills will take care of the work challenges and the work results.

His people know this about Robert and enjoy working for him. Some have followed him to new companies because they know they will continue to be developed and grow. Robert's clear purpose attracts followers. In addition to making him more influential, his clear purpose simplifies his own leadership. Robert's decisions are clearly guided by his purpose. When faced with a major company decision, he looks for the impact on profit and growth, but he also looks at how the company's leadership capacity will be strengthened or diminished by the decision. His clear purpose gives him confidence in tough situations.

As an example, when the company needed a new Vice President of Global Sales, Robert surprised his peers by proposing his most talented direct report, Chris. Chris was integral to the success of the Operations unit that she was currently running for him and this move meant he would lose Chris from his organization. In addition, on paper Chris did not appear to have the same depth of direct sales experience as others. However, she had proven herself as an outstanding leader of several different types of business units and had a keen understanding of sales drivers.

Robert believed that the sales function needed fresh, inspiring leadership more than it needed technical sales input. He also saw the lateral move for Chris as a huge leap in her development for future, broader leadership positions. Even though it meant that Robert had the extra burden of replacing Chris in her current critical role, he pushed his recommendation for her to have the new job. Chris went on to increase global sales and her own exposure for future, larger assignments. Robert was satisfied that he had been true to his purpose of building leaders.

Benefits of Clear Purpose

Leaders sometimes do not see the direct connection between having clarity of purpose and having a confident presence that influences people. However, when you know why you are in a leadership position, and when you are clear about the purpose of your contribution, then you overcome fear and tentativeness as a leader. Being clear about your purpose reminds you of the bigger game that you care so deeply about. Then you have the courage to withstand the anxiety and risk that often come with making your contribution. When you don't remember your purpose, or have not identified it, you will be more easily overwhelmed by the daily stress of leadership.

Unclear Purpose: Sam

Sam was Vice President of Operations in a pharmaceutical company where he led a group of highly paid and highly trained technical specialists. Over the year that Sam had been in charge, complaints had been rising from the staff that Sam was too harsh. He barked orders, was critical of the work product and only talked to people when he needed an update on a project. Although the staff members agreed that Sam was brilliant in his personal technical expertise, many no longer wanted to work for him and turnover had begun to rise. Because the function is so highly specialized, people with this training are difficult to find, making turnover a serious threat to revenue.

When I started coaching Sam, my first question was: "Why do you want to be a leader?" Sam said he enjoyed being an expert at this technical function and felt he had the best view of how to make the best product for customers. Since that didn't really speak to leadership, my second question was more direct. I let a moment pass and then asked: "Why should people want to follow you?" Silence. Sam admitted that he did not have an answer for that question. He had not yet identified a clear purpose for himself as a leader, versus his purpose as a technical expert.

Much of Sam's abrupt style was based on the fact that his focus was only on the quality of the work and not on a larger purpose of why he became a leader of people (versus a leader of projects). Sam's focus in coaching was to get clear about what leadership of human beings really means and to see if he had a purpose that was going to contribute to that.

As Sam worked through his true feelings about his purpose, he was able to identify the one thing he cared about most. His purpose was to raise the quality of clinical research everywhere. Once he identified that, the coaching focused on specific methods. How was he going to raise quality? In the end, Sam was able to see that in order to achieve this purpose that he cared deeply about, he would have to become more of a teacher and educator of others and thereby influence them to raise quality.

To see being a teacher as a major ingredient of his senior leadership role was a real paradigm shift for Sam. He had never viewed that as part of his job. This new realization laid the groundwork for him to start changing his behavior with people. He started practicing making space for people's questions, more regular one-on-one meetings with his reports, and more patient explanations of the context around projects. It was not an easy shift for Sam, but our coaching work helped remind him of his passion around his purpose— the reason to work on his new way of being.

53

Let Your Purpose Guide You

When you are clear about your purpose, it comes through in your presence. If people sense that you know where you're going and that you are passionate about getting there, you become very attractive as a leader. **Purpose fuels clarity.** Purpose helps people understand why a leader makes the decisions he or she makes.

Being able to clearly state your purpose will serve as your inner guidance, your compass, so that you always have a clear direction. *A clear purpose simplifies your leadership decisions and actions, especially when things get tough.* Purpose helps you feel confident that you know the right thing to do, because you feel it in your gut. Declaring your purpose will guide you in how you use your power. Purpose will have you step beyond your fears, persevere even when you make mistakes, and go to sleep at night feeling fulfilled.

Your purpose is what you will return to when you feel discouraged, tired or lost, as leaders often do. Purpose boosts your spirits so that you can stay the course when challenged. Declaring your purpose makes you a true player — someone who fully participates in life. Then, as you consider different actions, you will only need to ask: *"How does this align with my purpose?"* Your purpose shapes your life.

Identifying Your Purpose

There are many ways to identify your purpose. Some leaders intuitively know their purpose. Others read books to identify or discover their purpose or mission or calling. More structured learning options for clarifying one's purpose include attending training seminars that focus on purpose, personal development training, or working with a coach who specializes in purpose. Whatever method you choose, some key guidelines will make identifying your purpose easier and faster.

➤ **Purpose is not intellectual.** When you are in touch with your purpose, you will know because you will have feelings and emotions associated with it. Since purpose is about your passion, purpose is often reflected in the memories you have of the times you felt most excited about your work and your life.

➤ **Purpose does not have to be written in a perfect vision or mission statement.** Vision and mission statements can be very helpful for clarity, but only if the statement is one that you actually remember and use on a daily basis. Too many of us have perfectly written vision or purpose statements that are in a drawer, or forgotten after we attend a vision retreat. To clarify your purpose, a short phrase that is meaningful to you and brings up your personal emotions and/or vivid image will be enough.

➤ **Purpose does not have to be identified as your one single purpose for all time.** Depending on several factors including specificity or broadness of one's purpose statement, life experiences, and life changes, purpose may shift and change over time. The way you summarize or talk about your purpose may change. Or you may identify a purpose for your whole life as well as a purpose for particular parts of your life, such as your purpose as a parent, your purpose as a leader, your purpose as a friend.

For example, Helen, one of the senior executives I coach, identified her life purpose as "helping people to be better people." She sees her overall life purpose played out in the different arenas of her life. She says that her purpose as a parent is to "raise children to be great people" and her purpose as a CEO is to "grow and develop leaders".

Your purpose only needs to be meaningful to you, not to anyone else. Start by focusing on what you feel your purpose is right now; you can add to it or revise it at anytime. Following are some examples from my clients. They are senior executive leaders who I admire and respect. These are their personal purposes specifically related to their own leadership, not their company's purpose or its vision statement. Each statement is what that leader values, cares deeply about and sees as their purpose as a leader. This is the reason they chose to step up to a leadership position. In some cases the leader may also have a broader life purpose of which this leadership purpose is a part.

Client examples: *"My purpose is to"*...

➤ *grow and develop leaders.*

➤ *teach people to accomplish more together than separately.*

➤ *help leaders maximize people's contributions.*

➤ *create interdisciplinary approaches to health problems.*

➤ *help mothers nourish new babies.*

➤ *teach companies how to make better decisions by managing risk.*

➤ *expand the growth of companies that do beneficial things for people.*

➤ *match great ideas with the right people and resources.*

➤ *accelerate the development of new cures for disease.*

➤ *teach companies how to treat consumers.*

➤ *help people save money to have a better life.*

➤ *improve the lives of disabled people.*

➤ *show companies how to use compensation plans as a strategic tool.*

➤ *help women succeed at senior levels of business.*

➤ *build teams of great thinkers who create solutions.*

➤ *teach people to accomplish things more easily.*

Each of the purposes listed above helps that leader clarify their overall direction as they lead. When the leader is deciding how to use their time, they ask if a given activity supports this one phrase that summarizes their purpose. When the leader feels the stress of senior leadership, they remind themselves of their one phrase of purpose. That helps them feel the reassurance that something deeply valued can bring. These short purpose statements help a leader guide their behavior, suggest how to solve problems, guide who to have relationships with, which meetings to attend, what perspective to have, strategies, policies and more. Coming back to your purpose clarifies a great many things.

How do you know if your own purpose is clear enough, or if it needs some work? My clients have taught me that the most influential leaders are able to answer questions about their purpose very specifically. See how satisfied you are with your own answers.

Assessing the clarity of your Purpose

How do you know how fully you have developed your Purpose? Here are some useful questions to ask yourself.

➤ Are you satisfied that you know why you want to be a leader versus an individual contributor?

➤ Can you state your purpose as a leader clearly in just a few sentences?

➤ How well does your purpose match your personal values?

➤ Is your purpose for being a leader challenging you to grow and develop all the time?

➤ How does your purpose as a leader benefit people around you?

➤ Do you demonstrate your purpose so well that others know what it is?

➤ How satisfied are you that your purpose as a leader is significant and meaningful for you?

... make things better

(• people
(• processes
(• company
(• leaders
(• myself

59

Purpose and The Influence Puzzle® Model

Purpose is the first of the three Ps and the first ingredient of a powerful and influential presence. As we work through The Influence Puzzle® Model, you will see that all pieces of the model work together to help you strengthen your presence. Purpose is intertwined with all the other ingredients:

➤ A clear Purpose motivates you to use your Power.

➤ Making decisions based on your Purpose supports you in feeling Peace.

➤ Your Purpose helps you create Clarity.

➤ Commitment to your Purpose supports your Courage.

➤ Living your Purpose expands your Connection.

My Own Journey to Purpose

People find their purpose in life in many different ways, and it is not always a linear, logical process. For me, my purpose became most clear in a moment that I can only describe as: I felt like I was on fire!

This happened a while back when I was still a corporate executive. I was managing a huge healthcare operation's staff of over 700 people. The job was exciting, very stressful, rewarding and relentless, all at the same time.

One day as part of my own ongoing leadership development, I attended a training class in New York City for leaders on how to motivate and empower the people you lead. The teacher stood on a circular stage, surrounded on three sides by an audience of several hundred. He was outstanding. I watched him move around the stage and connect with the audience in a way I had never seen before. He used very few props, slides or handouts; his presence itself was the teacher.

Best of all, his ideas about how to better manage people really made sense to me. I was already thinking of ways I could use what I was learning for my real work problems with my own staff. I remember feeling right then, "I want to do what this guy is doing." But my feeling was more of a wish, a "maybe someday" pleasant thought.

I returned to my corporate job energized. I immediately went to see our internal HR people to tell them we had to hire the training class teacher to come to our office to train all 700 of my staff. I explained that the class would help the staff understand motivation and empowerment for themselves.

However, I was told that there was no budget for that type of training. Our training dollars were already assigned for technical healthcare staff training. I was really disappointed but I believed in the idea, so I said, "Then I'll do the training myself."

I knew I couldn't duplicate the class, but I could give people a short summary of what I thought was so meaningful. So we organized voluntary, one-hour seminars called "Motivation and Empowerment" to be held at the end of the workday.

On the day of the first seminar, I sat in our conference room, waiting. I had expected some of my direct reports to attend, but was surprised and delighted as more and more people filed in. I shared everything I was excited about in this material, told them all about the class, and had them practice a few of the exercises I had learned.

My staff loved it. They were engaged, sharing their perspectives and asking questions. I was seeing real learning happening, live. I repeated these small group seminars several times over a week or so, and I got better at my ability to share the concepts. People were excited and talking with each other about the material. Some stayed after class to talk with me, their faces more alive than usual at work.

During my last presentation, I was so engrossed in my staff's learning that I forgot myself. I was completely interested in their questions. I was fascinated by questions like, how could I better explain the concepts? How could I help them get that "aha" feeling that I got when I learned the material? What could I say to help them make their jobs easier? And in that moment of forgetting me and being excited to help all of us learn together, I felt so involved, so motivated, that I felt like I was on fire! Call it passion or enthusiasm — it was thrilling. What I felt about presenting these training seminars and helping people learn things that they really found helpful was, "I was born to do this." For me, that was life showing me a major part of my purpose.

In that moment I took a big step forward in clarity around my purpose. I think your purpose can change at different points in your life, but for me, at that point, I learned that my purpose had something to do with helping corporate leaders in a practical way so that their jobs as leaders became easier. My purpose seemed to be helping leaders suffer less and evolve upward. Overall, my purpose seemed to be helping corporate America become a better place.

After the last person left my class, I turned off the lights and started walking toward the escalator to leave the building. And I knew something significant was happening. I still felt so "on fire" that I was afraid to tell anyone! It felt weird to be that excited.

I knew that someday I would be helping people learn like this, not in the traditional way, but in the way I had just experienced, where everyone was excited. But how? I had worked my whole life to be a successful corporate executive. And I had made it to this big job. How could I leave this? Where did this new excitement fit in?

I walked to my car amazed by what I was feeling. At that moment, I didn't know how I would experience this again. But I knew I would. I just knew.

The 3 Ps of Leadership

POWER *n.* the ability to act or perform effectively; strength capable of being exerted

> *"Real power does not allow the birth of an enemy."*
>
> *— AUTHOR UNKNOWN*

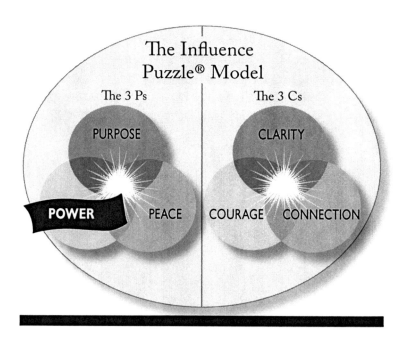

The Influence Puzzle® Model

The 3 Ps

PURPOSE

POWER   PEACE

The 3 Cs

CLARITY

COURAGE   CONNECTION

POWER

Demonstrate the right use of your Power

If you want powerful influence that comes from your strong personal presence, the next aspect of presence to develop is your Power.

What Is Power?

It may seem as if power comes from a senior executive title or from the authority you have to approve or stop business initiatives. But when you consider what really motivates people to do things in an organization, it becomes clear that *real power is the ability to influence people to act— not because they have to, but because they believe in you and are convinced that it's a great idea.*

Your power is your ability to perform effectively, to make happen what you intend to happen. In spite of the organizational chart, no one can give you real power. Real power is something you decide to have and decide how to use. Power is a key part of presence. When people feel your power, it is reassuring because the presence of your power reminds people that things are happening, that things will get done. When people experience that you are using your power deliberately and well, they feel that it's OK to put their faith in you. They are also more courageous. When people are afraid of moving forward, your powerful presence as a leader may be the key to encouraging them to take a step forward.

The Right Use of Power

To be a successful senior executive leader you need to be comfortable with power. You must use it well, and have that power be felt and experienced by others. Like many aspects of executive presence, power is very attractive, particularly when a leader uses their power at the right level, neither over- nor under-using it. *An influential leader demonstrates "the right use of power."*

Overusing power is using unnecessary force to get things done. Under-using power is holding back the strength required to get things done. The right use of your power is using your talent, ability, leverage, energy and attention in a way that matches the people involved and the situation so that the job gets done effectively. *Right use of power is also defined as using your power in a way that is in total alignment with your purpose and your values.* Right use of power can make the difference between your success and your failure. People are drawn to leaders who use power skillfully.

In order for power to be part of your presence, that power has to come from within you. People sense internal power. It is easy for people to see the difference between a leader who wields power because of the authority of a job position and a leader whose power radiates from inner confidence.

People tend to feel safer and do more for leaders who radiate appropriate power through their presence.

Overusing Power: Wayne

As VP of Sales and a 10-year veteran in software solutions, Wayne is a tremendous asset when the company needs to close a sale. However, Wayne has gotten feedback from his peers that is now raising questions about his longer-term ability to lead. His peers say that Wayne is great when things are going well but when the team has business problems to solve together, Wayne is often impatient with the group. He can be condescending and critical of his peers' ideas, frequently pointing out that the team is not as effective at sales and marketing as it needs to be.

Although Wayne says that he is only pointing out the team's flaws because customers are demanding more, his peers feel that Wayne uses customer information as an excuse to criticize others. Wayne will go to great length to talk about why a peer's idea won't work, but he does not offer any specific recommendations on what the team could do instead. Wayne is being groomed for the next level, but now the Board has heard of his peers' concerns and wonder if they will follow him if he becomes their boss.

The strategy for coaching Wayne was to develop new ways for managing his own frustration. Interestingly, Wayne came to see that his definition of executive leadership needed to be expanded. Like so many executives, Wayne had been promoted based on his outstanding technical ability — in this case, his sales ability.

Once he reached VP level, other leadership competencies were expected, and were included on his performance evaluation. However, Wayne had been given little attention to help him develop essential senior executive skills such as aligning a team, collaborating, influencing others and developing people. **Wayne had to recognize that his ability to help his peers and move the team forward was just as important as closing sales.** Wayne would have to change the way he operated: from using his power to criticize to using his power to encourage.

Coaching was the catalyst for some very deep personal work for Wayne. He did some soul searching to be sure that he really wanted to be a senior executive sales leader versus a very high-level individual salesperson. Companies often assume that this decision has already been made if a person has reached VP level. However, many high achievers are so focused on great performance and advancement that they often do not give themselves a chance to really ask the question: Do I want to use my power to lead others?

Under-using Power: Barbara

Barbara is VP of Finance for a large insurance company. She was promoted through the ranks quickly because of her strong financial acumen and her ability to walk people through the numbers in a clear and easy way. Barbara's current career goal is to broaden her experience by running a business unit, so she has been volunteering to lead special project teams to demonstrate her leadership ability. Due to the nature of the special projects, Barbara presents monthly updates to the CEO, COO and CFO.

And now, for the first time in her career, Barbara has hit a wall in her own performance. When she gets in front of the C-level team she becomes tentative in her presentation. She has gotten feedback that she appears unsure of herself and does not give a feeling of strong confidence about what's happening with the project. The CEO commented that Barbara seemed more confident when he first met her years ago as a management intern.

Barbara's coaching focus was to examine how she under-used her power. Barbara was able to see that she was putting too much pressure on herself by thinking that every C-level presentation was an evaluation of her worthiness to lead a business unit. She was choking under the self-created pressure. Barbara's key realization was that she was **using her power to focus on the wrong thing at the wrong time.** During the special project C-level update, she was focused on her internal questions and doubts about her own performance, rather than delivering the update.

The shift for Barbara was to stay in the present moment and use the C-level presentation to focus only on the task at hand, which was walking the meeting attendees through the project status. She had to see that it really was not about her in that moment; it was only about the audience and how she could help them do what they had asked her to do — walk them through what was happening with the business project. Once Barbara shifted her focus to that, her C-level presentations dramatically improved.

Assessing where you are with your own Power

How do you know how fully you have developed your Power? Here are some useful questions to ask yourself.

➤ How comfortable are you with using power?

➤ What would you say is the right use of your power?

➤ Are you using your power at your full potential? How do you know? What indicators support your opinion/ assessment?

➤ How satisfied are you that you have stepped up to new levels of power each time you take on a new assignment?

➤ How closely do you match your own ideal vision of a powerful person?

➤ Do others view you as a powerful leader?

➤ How satisfied are you with your level of personal confidence in life, not just on the job?

➤ How comfortably do you demonstrate power, even in the presence of people you perceive to be more powerful than you?

My Own Journey to Power

If I had to summarize the most valuable lesson I have learned about power in my own life, it would be this: Stay in the present moment; that is where my power is. Being powerful means being fully present with the person or situation that is in front of me. I have learned that it's difficult to say exactly what "using one's power fully" looks like. There is no specific description or list of the correct ways to be powerful. Power happens in the moment, is specific to the individual, and comes from inside.

I was once a student in a personal development training class with a small group of seven other students. (Although I often present seminars myself, I enjoy taking seminars as a student just as much.) Our task in this class was to discuss the material until all eight students understood it. Only then could we, as a team, move on to the next part of the class.

I have to admit, I was not happy to be learning in a team situation. I'm pretty independent, so I felt I could move faster on my own. From the start, I felt my group was moving too slowly. In an effort to be helpful, I placed my watch in the middle of the table and pointed out how much time the group was taking to do the exercise. I did this about every five minutes and, needless to say, the group did not find my reminders helpful. Obnoxious? Yes. Helpful? No. I was growing more impatient and more frustrated as different group members asked questions about things that I thought were not important and taking us totally off track.

Finally, after about 40 minutes, my own thoughts

were completely judgmental. In my head, I was calling my group a bunch of losers who were holding me back. I was talking to myself about how unfair this situation was because I had paid money to attend the class and now my progress was being held up by people I had never even met before. It was a multi-day workshop; if we couldn't get through this, we'd be behind the whole time. My self-talk went on and on about how the other people did not get it at all, I was infinitely smarter than they were, I certainly did not belong in this group... blah, blah, blah.

So I got up from the table, found one of the instructors and announced to her, "I'd like to be assigned to a new group." The instructor had seen my type of arrogance before. She smiled slightly. She pleasantly said there would be no changing groups. I got more agitated because she apparently did not understand how important my issue was. I explained to her how much more intelligent I was than everyone else in my group; how I grasped things faster and how I deserved special treatment. The instructor listened to me fully, smiled again, and was unimpressed. She repeated in a pleasant voice that there would be no changing groups. Then she sat down with me and gave me some excellent advice.

"Val, you are using all your power to point out what's wrong with your group and what's wrong with the process, and to criticize how slowly they are moving," she said quietly. "You are not even in the room with your group. You are in your head, worried about the future outcome, worried about when the group will finish and how that will impact you.

"What if you used your power differently to actually help the group? Since you believe you are so smart, how could you use your power to do your part to help the entire group understand the material? Then wouldn't the group naturally move faster?"

I didn't like the instructor's advice at all (clearly she did not see my superiority). But there was something about her quiet, confident power that got my attention. And I could see she was not going to put me in another group.

So I stomped back to my group. No one was thrilled at my return.

At first I sat there with my arms folded. I was there under protest. But then I started to actually see my own arrogance, and I also realized my self-righteous position just did not feel good, even to me. Since I had no choice, I decided to shift. I began to join the discussion, to help clarify the questions that people were asking. I asked my own questions, too. I started facilitating versus criticizing. I started listening and learning new aspects of the material. I stayed in the moment, connecting to the other people, responding to whatever came up in the present instead of worrying about the future outcome. And to my amazement, as the instructor predicted, the group started moving faster. We successfully completed the exercise in a reasonable time. Amazing.

I learned a few things that day about the "right use of power." Initially, I had misdirected my power when I was concerned only about my own needs and my own progress. Even though my judgments were not always said aloud and were largely in my head, overall, I had used my power to put my group down and to elevate myself. I rationalized what I was doing by feeling that I was protecting myself. It felt reasonable to try to control the situation so that I would have a good end result. But now I could see that using my power in this way, to protect myself from a minor inconvenience at the expense of others, is really a very small game. I had become good at this game, but even I could see that it was a small game.

Later, after the instructor helped me, I used my power in a much better way: in service of the total team and in the present moment. The result was that I also benefited more. I realized that maybe I wasn't as smart as I had thought.

The times when I am most powerful are when I am connected with the people in front of me and responding to the reality of what is actually happening versus my idea of what I think should be happening. A question that I try to ask myself is about my true intention: What am I really trying to do here? Is this the right use of my power? Not just for me, but for everyone involved?

Sometimes the question of how best to use power is internal: How do I use my power on my own behalf, when I need it to help myself with myself? How do I make sure that I am not *under*-using my power?

I learned a little about this one day when I experienced severe stage fright. I had been a seminar leader and speaker for many years. But when I started to experience a little success, there came a time that my normal small nervousness before going on stage became a huge anxiety and a real obstacle.

I was about to speak before about 250 people at a corporate event in a New York City hotel. It was the first time I had spoken publicly about some of my basic beliefs that later led to the model in this book. My speaking on stage suddenly felt a lot more personal, and I felt a lot more exposed. These were not just broadly accepted views on leadership. I was talking about my own specific philosophy and recommendations on leadership.

I was waiting in the wings of the stage while a colleague was talking to the audience to introduce me. I'd had a good breakfast, I felt comfortable that I was well dressed, and I had practiced the presentation backwards and forwards. I was completely prepared. I had about five minutes before going on. That's when my stage fright, which had been building for the last hour or so, took a surprising form.

I was standing there feeling very anxious and breathing a lot. I saw that I would have to walk up four or five steps to reach the stage, and then walk about six feet to the center of the stage. At that moment I felt a searing, sharp pain in my right leg from my ankle through my calf up to the back of my knee. I was having the type of painful muscle spasm that as kids we used to call a "charley horse." I was stunned. "What? Now?" I thought. "I never get charley horses and I am having one now?" I couldn't move my leg!

I started to panic because I could hear that the person introducing me was nearing the end of his remarks. I felt horror that my career was going to end right there in the wings because I wouldn't be able to get to the stage. I would also die of embarrassment. And I felt internally humiliated because I had a vague idea that my own fear was the cause of this sudden leg disability.

That is when another part of my consciousness kicked in. I could hear myself talking to myself, saying something like: "You worked so hard preparing for this moment. This was months of work to get you here, and now you are going to miss your moment over a painful but temporary physical condition? What about how deeply you cared about making this contribution?"

And while my internal conflict was going back and forth, my own power finally surfaced to win the debate. My power felt like an internal voice that said to me: "We are NOT going to miss this moment. If we have to drag our leg onto that stage, we are going. If we have to ask someone to carry us to the stage, we are going. If they have to put a chair in the middle of the stage and we have to give this speech sitting down, we will. But we are going to give this speech ... on this stage ... today ... to this audience!" I could actually feel the power come up from my own belly.

And then I did not care how bad it would look to limp up the stairs to the stage or how it would look to have to sit in a chair. I was going.

Meanwhile, I heard my colleague ending the introduction: "Now let's give a warm round of applause to welcome Val." I took the first step, feeling the pain in my leg. It hurt, but I took the next step. I felt supported by the audience's warm welcome. When I held the railing to take the first step to the stage, I was prepared to ask for help up the stairs. But my leg was suddenly fine. The muscle spasm was gone. I mounted the stairs and walked to the center of the stage.

Surprisingly, I had used my power on my own behalf! I learned that I had more power inside myself than I realized, and that I had been under-using my power before. I realized that I could direct my power. I was so grateful to make it to that stage, so surprised that I had gotten through my own fear, that I felt like a winner just to be standing there.

That day I gave one of the best speeches of my career.

The 3 Ps of Leadership

PEACE *n.* inner contentment, calm, serenity; harmonious relations

> *"If you want peace, stop fighting. If you want peace of mind, stop fighting with your thoughts."*
>
> — *PETER McWILLIAMS*

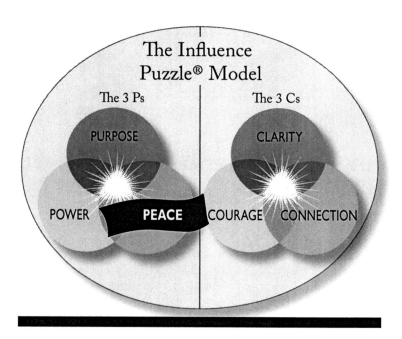

PEACE

Find the Peace that creates conditions for creativity and innovation

What Is Peace?

In order to be successful, a senior executive has to be able to help the people he or she leads be creative and innovative. When people have a basic feeling of peace, they are in a good position to release their unique creativity and new ideas. If you as a leader are going to help others feel peaceful, you will need to have your own internal sense of peace. When you have this internal peace, people feel it when they are with you. And that feeling impacts them. *Your peace is another aspect of your being that can powerfully influence others.*

So, for an executive leader, what is peace? You may think that having peace of mind means having the job you want, the money you want, and the friends and contacts that you want. But inner peace is actually a state of being that successful leaders develop so that they have peace of mind regardless of external situations. *In a corporation if you depend on external circumstances for inner peace or happiness, you will be at the mercy of whatever happens on a daily basis.* It is very difficult to base your internal peace on an ever-changing organizational environment. Peace of mind is something that you cultivate by making a personal decision that your source of peace is within you.

Peace is the feeling of inner contentment. Peace is feeling good about who you are as a person and who you are as a leader. Peace is feeling that the relationships you build are based on the intention to collaborate, to be straight with people, to contribute to the greater good. Peace is the feeling of harmony both inside yourself and outside with others. And contrary to popular belief, peace is not wimpy. It takes a powerful person to choose to be peaceful, especially in the face of difficult situations.

Benefits of Peace

It may seem that peace is a passive component to presence. Initially, I wondered myself: How can you be peaceful while achieving outstanding results? The idea of peace did not seem to fit with the fast pace of executive leadership. If you are peaceful, does that mean you are not guarding the fort? Not ready, therefore vulnerable? Does peace mean that you are weak? Not achieving? Boring? I had all these questions.

However, I have learned that peace is actually a strong foundation for powerful presence. Peace allows you to feel relaxed even during activity, balanced even when busy, whole even when managing several priorities. When you have peace of mind, you have the ability to sit still and be creative. You can see solutions to problems that you cannot see when you are in turmoil. *Peace is an excellent condition for a solution-oriented mind, for creativity and innovation. You see more. You know more.* And with that broader awareness, you actually are ready for whatever comes up. So instead of being more vulnerable, you are, in fact, better prepared to handle the unexpected in a calm way. You still achieve goals, but without the frenetic quality.

And the concern about becoming boring? My clients who have developed more peace are much more available to other people. Peaceful leaders tend to be more present when they speak to people. And people feel the impact of receiving the leader's full attention. People find peaceful leaders much more interesting and more attractive.

When a leader's presence communicates peace, people are encouraged. People feel relaxed and safe and reassured when they're in the presence of a peaceful leader. A peaceful presence becomes a strategic tool to motivate people to go beyond their current level of performance or to risk taking on new challenges. Peace is the aspect of presence that prompts people to tell the leader the truth about what's really going on, because they can trust that leader will not overreact or kill the messenger.

Peace and Strong Leadership

The leader who has developed peace is also still capable of handling the tough side of leadership. This is where the 3Ps of The Influence Puzzle® Model come together. The leader who has peace effectively employs power. This leader gives negative feedback when called for. They hold people accountable for performance. They confront the issues that are not being spoken about in meetings. They enforce their boundaries. They do the practical, tough things leaders do.

The leader whose power is based on peace cuts expenses, eliminates waste, and makes hard decisions about people and jobs. The difference between this leader and others is that he or she does all these challenging leadership tasks without becoming overly agitated. There is a difference between "responding" to business problems and "reacting" to business problems. The leader with a strong presence is in response, not reaction, mode.

Peace helps a leader project a serene and thoughtful presence that invites followers. Inner peace radiates outer confidence, the sense that all is well. People find such peace attractive in a leader and want to be a part of that stabilizing, reassuring force. Peace creates follower-ship. Being at peace is a very high state.

Peace is Self-Acceptance

It took me a very long time to learn that a major ingredient to having peace is self-acceptance. As a successful Executive Vice President recently said to me: "It's OK to be me. In fact, the only way I want to be is to be totally me. And if being me means that things work out, great! But if being me means that things don't work out, that's fine, too." This level of authenticity is based on profound self-acceptance. This client went on to say, *"One of the mistakes I made earlier in my career was thinking that I had to be someone else to be successful."*

As with most high achievers, senior leaders quite easily fall into the practice of living up to other people's expectations instead of their own. In fact, throughout our early careers, we were rewarded for meeting the standards of others: the boss, the customer, the Board.

This is fine as long as your personal standards are the same as those of your stakeholders. Unfortunately, many leaders get caught in a loop that looks something like this: High-achiever leaders lose touch with their own standards. They then spend a huge amount of energy trying to meet what they perceive as the expected external standards. They judge themselves harshly as not measuring up, thereby eroding their self-acceptance and their own confidence. And once that happens, they have no peace. *Without internal peace, it becomes very difficult for the leader to project the type of calm, confident presence that influences people.* And without becoming aware of the self-defeating loop, leaders limit their peace, presence and influence.

Reaction Mode: Obstacle to Peace

A major obstacle to a leader's peace is our human tendency to overreact. Going into reaction mode stems from our wanting to see things only from our own point of view and then being annoyed when others do not share our view. The tendency to look at the world through our own perspective, our own lens, is what makes up our own "story."

This is where the philosophy of Ontological Coaching is a useful tool.* Ontological Coaching focuses on how we

---

* Ontological Coaching was founded by Fernando Flores. Julio Olalla, founder of the Newfield Network, has been one of the major developers of Ontological Coaching).

perceive the world, and how our way of perceiving the world shapes our behavior and our experience of the world.

Our perspective, or our "story," is the sum total of our beliefs, opinions, experiences, memories and conclusions about any given subject. We have thousands, maybe millions, of stories playing in our heads about various things. We have stories about how we view our careers, stories about what we deserve in life, stories about our finances, our relationships, etc. We have stories about other people and their intentions toward us. And most importantly, we have stories about ourselves.

In short, we react to an event because we have created a story for ourselves about what that event means about life and a story about what that event means about us. *Having a story is like wearing colored sunglasses. If your glasses are orange, the world looks orange. If your glasses are blue, the world looks blue.* One key to life is to remember not to argue about whether the world is orange or blue. The key is to realize that you are wearing orange glasses versus assuming that you are actually seeing reality. *You are seeing life as you perceive it through your particular lenses.*

This story concept becomes a valuable tool for leaders when they use it to both understand their own reactions and to reduce the intensity and frequency of reacting. For example, when you feel stuck in life, it is often because you are stuck in an old story that you won't let go of. It feels as if you have no choice, or you can't change. But that is just the nature of being in your story (or having on orange sunglasses). Once you change your story about a situation or a person, life can look a lot different and you are no longer stuck.

The Old Way: The Caveman Approach to Executive Development

A major part of what makes executive coaching so powerful for a leader's development is that a coach can help a leader shift from old stories about their limitations to new stories about their capabilities. At the higher levels, "leadership skill training" alone is simply not enough to develop powerful influence.

Sometimes leaders try to rush through their development. They say to the coach: "Just tell me what to do to influence my people better. Just give me the steps." And if the leader focuses on remembering a few skill tips and practices them diligently, their performance will improve somewhat for a short time. But this is a mechanical approach to behavior change. It takes a huge amount of energy for the leader to remember, focus, and practice. It readily is perceived by others as a "technique". It is the old way, the caveman approach to executive development.

The new way, and the much easier way, draws on Ontological Coaching: help the leader change their story. *Help the leader fundamentally look at things differently. Then their behavior changes almost automatically, effortlessly.* The leader will not need to work so hard to remember tips or focus or practice because their big-picture perspective has changed. And behavior flows from one's overall perspective. Change the perspective and the behavior will follow.

A *Vice President's Story*

I once coached a Vice President of Products for a technology consulting company who presented as confident, engaging and quite inspiring in our initial meeting. Mitch was well thought of and the company rated him highly. Clearly he would be promoted. However, there was one key area for development. In spite of his great and outgoing personality when interacting with peers and senior management, Mitch was viewed by his staff as somewhat distant, not easy to approach and not very motivating. This sometimes resulted in lower productivity than he felt his team was capable of. The team certainly spent too much of their time talking to each other about their concerns with Mitch's style. The team also did not feel comfortable sharing some of their obstacles with him, so problems took longer than expected to solve.

During coaching, Mitch was able to clearly identify a fundamental story that he held about being a leader. His story was based on difficulties with giving tough feedback to direct reports when they had a performance problem. In past experiences where he had close relationships with his direct reports, the closeness itself made it much harder for him to give difficult feedback. It felt to Mitch as if he was being the bad guy to a friend. In fact, those past direct reports had told Mitch that he *was* being the bad guy. The strategy he had developed over the years for handling this problem was to not get very close to direct reports. Mitch felt it was easier to stay distant so that when it was time to review performance, he would have no conflict.

Our work in coaching was for Mitch to let go of his old story, starting with updating his definition of what it means to have a good relationship with a direct report versus a friendship. We outlined clear differences. We also worked on appropriate boundaries for the work relationship so that Mitch could bring his naturally excellent interpersonal skills into play while staying clear with direct reports on the respective roles of leader and direct report. Once Mitch shifted his story, he no longer had concerns around being viewed as the bad guy.

Mitch's new story included the value of providing tough feedback so that people grow and develop. To his credit, Mitch's behavior changed almost overnight. He dropped by people's desks, was available to go out to lunch, and asked for people's ideas informally. We did a repeat 360-degree evaluation, which validated that the staff saw and appreciated the changes. The best part was that Mitch felt more natural with his way of being with people. His new story, with its new definitions and new boundaries, helped him relax and be more effective. Mitch did not have to work very hard on specific behaviors or have a checklist for new things to try. He fundamentally viewed things differently and his behavior flowed naturally from that changed view.

One key to developing true peace as a person, and as a successful senior leader, is to develop the ability to identify your stories and change them intentionally.

How the 3 Ps of the Puzzle Work Together

As we look at the 3 Ps, the sweet spot of powerful presence is where all three, Purpose, Power and Peace, overlap. All parts of the puzzle need to fit together. When we don't have peace, we are distracted and out of internal alignment. That means we are not using our power to the fullest extent because some of our power is being lost fulfilling another purpose. Instead of aligning all available power to act on what we have stated as our purpose, some of our power is diverted to proving ourselves to other people.

The greatest and most influential presence is developed when we practice all 3 Ps: Purpose, Power and Peace simultaneously.

The 3 Ps Overlap: Mike

A typical example is Mike, who is a very competent financial leader, but has difficulty selling his ideas to his marketing peers at large open staff meetings. In short, he has assumptions about the expectations of seasoned marketing people. He thinks they expect him to give a super polished presentation, as they would do. But he is a finance guy and the perfect presentation is not who he is.

Unfortunately, in trying to live up to his own perception of what he thinks his marketing peers' expectation is, he has made himself anxious and not peaceful. Therefore, he is tentative in using his power and has difficulty carrying out his purpose. All 3 Ps — Purpose, Power and Peace —are connected, and since he is not at peace, all three are affected.

So what's the connection between cultivating more peace in one's life and having more power. Successful leaders have learned that when they have peace of mind and can think clearly in a relaxed way, they generate more ideas for better strategies. Better strategies help them use power more wisely, giving choices more impact. When peaceful, leaders make better decisions. By contrast, a mind in turmoil has difficulty making any decision at all.

A personal commitment to peace helps you trust yourself as you take on higher levels of responsibility and wield greater power. If peace is one of your core values, you will not have to worry about misusing your power or getting caught up in your own ego. Your dedication to cultivating peace even when demonstrating power helps balance your leadership style, knowing when to be firm and when to ease up. *Peace and Power go hand in hand to support the effective execution of a leader's Purpose.*

An Example of Peace: Stan

Stan is the CEO of a publishing company that has grown significantly over the past 15 years. Stan is not the stereotypical image of a CEO: he is fairly quiet in a group meeting; an average-looking, middle-aged man with glasses.

Stan started his career as a teacher who branched out into writing and gradually expanded a tiny company into a substantial one. Stan has peace. He is a thoughtful person who listens attentively to his management team. He encourages their ideas through asking questions about their thinking. He is a learner *with* his people, often nodding his head in agreement, smiling and quietly noting their suggestions. Stan is a relaxed guy who speaks in an even tone, often sits back with his feet on the desk, and takes time for long coffee breaks to discuss new plans. Stan uses all his vacation time; he is sometimes completely unavailable by cell phone, has hobbies unrelated to the business, and shares openly how much he works on his own ongoing development.

People feel calm in Stan's presence and seek out his mentorship. His senior leaders look forward to reviewing work with him because they feel inspired after discussing projects with him, even though he asks many more questions than he gives answers. For all these reasons, people have followed Stan over the years and the company has grown both in revenue and in size. Stan is someone people want to emulate. In his quiet, peaceful way he is a very powerful leader of a successful organization.

Peace is a Solution for Work-Life Balance

If you are struggling with work-life balance, chances are you have not fully cultivated inner peace. Work-life balance problems mean that there is some internal struggle or judgment about how you are living. When you have peace, you let go of those self-criticisms and accept the choices that you have made, knowing that you can change your choices at any time. Peace is balance. Peace is letting go of the need to do it all and do it all perfectly. You know you have developed peace when you no longer multitask as a way of life, when you stop over-scheduling yourself, when you no longer carry over vacation days, and when you can pause before over-reacting.

Assessing your inner Peace

How do you know how fully you have developed your inner Peace? Here are some useful questions to ask yourself.

➤ How satisfied are you that you live a balanced life?

➤ What kinds of things do you do that would have others see you as peaceful?

➤ How well do you stay calm in a conflict situation?

➤ How satisfied are you with your ability to stay out of reaction mode?

➤ How easy do you find it to relax when you're not working?

➤ Have you overcome the drive to multitask constantly?

➤ How comfortable are you with turning off your BlackBerry®?

➤ How well do you accept circumstances that you cannot control?

My Own Journey to Peace

Since I am an overachiever, finding peace has been, and still is, a huge challenge for me. But I have learned some things that make it a lot easier to be peaceful.

For most of my life, I have believed that life is tough, so I have to be tougher. Especially as a corporate executive, I believed in being a warrior in business and wearing lots of armor to survive. My philosophy had been: move fast, don't let anyone get too close, and keep your guard up at all times.

The corporate environment is so relentless, so challenging, that it seems counterintuitive to suggest peace as a success factor for senior leaders. But I have seen in my own life that as I've practiced being more relaxed, warmer, even softer, my power and confidence have increased. The paradox is this: As I let down layers of my armor, it seems to enhance my strength. After all, powerful, strong people don't feel it necessary to walk around with eight layers of armor. I also learned that when I am more peaceful and confident, I don't have to view every challenging event as a reason to go to war.

A key tool for developing my peace is what I have learned about handling stressful events: It is not what happens to you in life; it is how you react to it. Reactions, especially my overreactions, are what disturb my peace of mind. So another key to peace for me has been learning and practicing how to reduce my overreactions and to recover quickly when I do react.

When it came to peace, initially I had a difficult time seeing that I could be any part of my own problem. I didn't see that I had any of my own "stories" about stressful events. I assumed that I knew "the truth" of the event. In fact, I would have listed for you all the people who were at the root of any problem I had. I really believed that "if it were not for this person doing that I would be happy and my problems would be solved." What I couldn't see was that I had a "story" about life and my role in life, and that story was causing me to overreact frequently.

One example was when I ordered a new patio table for my house from a local large department store. I spent a lot of time picking out the exact table, matching chairs and planning a delivery date since I was having a barbeque.

On the day before the scheduled delivery, I was at work when a woman from the department store called to say that the specific patio table I had ordered had been damaged, and instead, they would be sending another table that was the same style but was two feet larger, and it was on the way.

I immediately interrupted the woman with my most assertive voice. I took a huge breath and started speaking very fast to let her know that I was fully aware that the larger table cost two hundred dollars more than the smaller one, and that they were not going to take advantage of me ... because they damaged my table ... and that I was not going to buy a larger table ... and that they clearly had management problems to be calling the customer at the last minute .... I went on for a while.

Even though I was fairly polite in my language, I was cold, rigid and in full-blown reaction mode. I felt I knew exactly what this big department store was trying to pull: get more of my money and cover up their mistake. I also could feel myself gearing up for a fight. I was going to stand up to them and not let them get away with victimizing me. I was pretty worked up.

In the middle of my self-righteous monologue, the woman said, "Oh, you don't understand; we are calling to ask you if you are OK with a larger patio table, but at no cost to you since it was the company's error."

"Huh?" I was still suspicious.

I said, "So I get a bigger table for free?"

"Yes," she said.

I paused. I said, "So this is a good thing?"

"Yes," she said, "this is a good thing."

"Oh," I said. "Well in that case ... uh ... thank you. Yes, I accept." With that, all the wind went out of my sails. OK. No war after all. At least, no war today.

With the help of my own coach, I learned to see that this patio example was "my story." My story was that I am the "action hero," the "warrior," and I have to fight for justice for myself against the big, bad establishment. As my coach pointed out, I had already had similar struggles with the phone company, the insurance company and the electric company. Different situations, different people, but my story was the same: action hero at war.

Happily for me, my coach helped me create a new story. The new story became: there are times when I may have to assert myself to solve life's problems, but I do not have to be "typecast" as the perpetual action hero. Even Freud said, "Sometimes a cigar is just a cigar."

Being able to see my own "stories" as the root cause of my reactions has really helped me on the road to having more peace in my life. I am a work in progress, trying each day to live my new story.

My commitment was really put to the test some time later, when a close friend and colleague challenged me on making this shift.

We were at a retreat at a country home in the Napa Valley. It was just after lunch and about 10 of us were sitting in a relaxed circle of chairs on the lawn, in the sunshine. They were very close colleagues, so I was in a really supportive environment. I had been talking to the group about my efforts to live my new story and not always be the warrior. One of my friends looked right at me and slowly, but with some intensity, asked me a powerful question. He asked: "Val, are you willing to declare that the war is over?" The question stunned me. I know it sounds like a clear question, but I couldn't even say anything. He was asking me to really shift from one of my core ways of being.

When he saw that I was looking back at him like a deer in headlights, he added to the question. "Val, are you willing to declare that the war is over ... and that you won?" That question really landed for me. I exhaled and felt the relief.

"OK, yes," I said. "I can declare that." It was the bridge I needed. As part of my own transition to peace, I still needed to feel that I had won the war before I could start letting it go. I hope to evolve to the point where even the win won't matter so much; but I'm not there yet. Soon.

On a practical level, I have found that it is also useful to have some type of physical practice for peace.

The key practice for me has been meditation; nothing fancy, just simple breath meditation— watching the sensation of your breath at your nose as you inhale and exhale. There is no need for any special mantra or specific religious content; just slowing down the breath, which automatically slows down the mind. I have found that practicing meditative breathing, along with yoga, has helped my stress level significantly. Just 10 to 20 minutes in the morning has worked very well.

As my meditation teacher says, "Train your mind to be peaceful and that will inspire others to be peaceful. And in turn, they will inspire people they are in contact with to be peaceful. How wonderful if you yourself in this way could be the type of leader who inspires ripples of inner peace."

The 3 Cs for Leaders

CLARITY *n.* clearness; the quality or state of being easy to perceive; free from obscurity or confusion

"Simplicity is the ultimate sophistication."

– LEONARDO DA VINCI

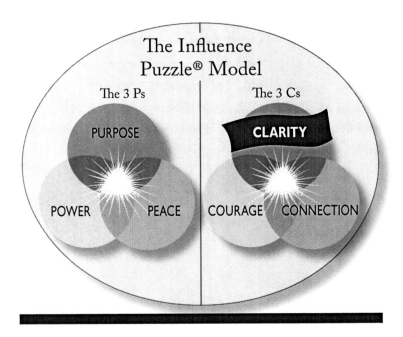

CLARITY

Create the Clarity that inspires people to follow.

What Is Clarity?

You may think that if your oral communication skills are good and you are articulate and a good speaker, you have clarity. However, clarity is not just about delivering your message, clarity is about how well your message is received by your audience.

Clarity is being certain, being free from doubt or confusion. Clarity is being straight with people and having people experience you as knowing what you want. Clarity comes from knowing your purpose. When you are clear about your purpose, you have direct access to what you believe in at the deepest level.

Clarity about What?

What specific things does a senior executive leader need to have clarity about? On the business side, some of these are obvious. As a leader you want to be clear about your vision or mission for the organization; the business strategies and plans; the revenue targets. You want to be sure that all members of your team are clear about those as well. You want to be sure that you create clarity about job roles and responsibilities, as well as clarity in your emails, voicemails and presentations.

But clarity about business is not enough. Successful leaders who are influential also have clarity around their personal presence. Are you clear about your personal standards and expectations? Your values? Your boundaries? Your needs? And do you make those personal preferences clear to others? Are you clear about your skills? Your contribution? Real clarity results in people being able to describe what you stand for and what you care about, because these things are so clear to them when they are in your presence.

Clarity in Action: Joyce

Joyce is Vice President of Marketing of a women's apparel company. She moved up to the senior ranks very quickly, largely because she is crystal clear about the contribution she makes to the company. Joyce is all about responsiveness to customers. She is known to be like a pit bull with her relentless questions about new product development. Like a constant campaign slogan, you can count on her to ask about any new product plan: "Show me the customer!" If the project matches a current customer need, she approves it and it gets funded; if not, she rejects it even if it is a good idea in theory.

Joyce's clarity about her customer orientation is reflected in many of her actions. She attends all large customer-facing events, even when it is inconvenient. She visits the company call centers just to listen to live customer calls. She has "Customer Insight Luncheons" once a month to share current and future expected customer trends. Because she has become expert at both knowing the pulse of the customer and being able to clearly summarize it for others, she adds great value to the company. People ask to work for Joyce because of her laser-like, clear focus.

As a person, Joyce is known to be equally clear. She puts issues on the table, she doesn't pull punches, she is direct without shutting people down. People call her "No Mystery Joyce" because she tells you exactly what she thinks—and what she thinks matches what she does. So although not everyone agrees with her, everyone does know where she stands and that makes her very attractive. People want her participation; they listen to her opinion. Joyce's presence influences people and thereby influences results.

Benefits of Clarity

When you, as a leader, have clarity, your communication is to the point and easy to "get." When you are clear, you make requests and present messages that are easily understood. When you are clear, your actions demonstrate what the priorities are and you handle things in a focused way.

Clarity is important for building an influential presence because most people are looking for a clear direction. When you can provide that clear direction, you have much more influence with the people who follow you. Clarity helps people trust you because they feel they know you. When you, as a leader, are clear, people understand who you are. People can see where you are leading them. This type of certainty is inspiring and helps people feel comfortable, particularly when you are leading them in a new direction.

Assessing your own Clarity

How do you know how fully you have developed your Clarity?
Here are some useful questions to ask yourself.

➤ As a leader, how clear is your vision and mission for the
business?

➤ How clearly do you demonstrate results?

➤ When you communicate in presentations or one-on-one,
how satisfied are you that you are crisp and clear?

➤ How well do you communicate your top three priorities
in business?

➤ How satisfied are you that you demonstrate your awareness
of the big picture?

➤ How clear are you on your criteria for making tough
business decisions?

➤ How satisfied are you that people know who you are and
what you stand for?

➤ How clearly can you assess other people's styles before you
decide how to approach them?

➤ How well do you know where you have blind spots?

➤ How clear are you on your personal standards? Personal
boundaries?

➤ In dealing with people, how comfortable are you at being
direct, even on sensitive topics?

Clarity and The Influence Puzzle®

Your clarity makes your presence more powerful, especially when clarity is blended with the other parts of The Influence Puzzle® Model. Start imagining yourself having several of the six parts of The Influence Puzzle® working together: Imagine that as a leader you know what your purpose is, you demonstrate the right use of your power, you radiate peace and you have clarity— both about the business and about who you are. With just these first four pieces of the puzzle, imagine how powerful your presence would be. Imagine how much your ability to influence would improve.

My Own Journey to Clarity

I realized pretty quickly that one of the main reasons I had difficulty being clear with other people was because I did not have enough clarity within myself. I did not have clear, specific answers for personal questions like:

➤ What are my personal standards?

➤ What work conditions do I need to perform at my best?

➤ What exactly are my boundaries?

➤ What is not OK with me?

➤ Who gets to be in my inner circle and hang out with me?

➤ What do I need in a colleague relationship?

➤ What really makes me happy?

These were things I just had not given a lot of thought to. But these are the kinds of things that form the foundation for personal confidence and being clear on who you are. (This is Personal Foundation work and one of the first areas I worked on as a client with my own coach.*)

Once I was able to clearly identify my preferences — what I value, what does not work for me, what I truly need in a project, a relationship, a friend or a job — once I really knew that, it was very easy to be clear with other people.

In the beginning, however, demonstrating clarity with people can feel risky, especially when work and money are involved. An example is my own story of "a path not taken."

When I started my business, like many consultants, I worked with anyone who would hire me to do pretty much anything. As my clarity grew, I could see that I really did have a preferred type of work and type of client. My favorite experiences seemed to be with corporate executives in leadership positions with large companies, often high-achieving, challenging clients who needed a customized approach. I had gotten clear that the specific types of leadership development I enjoy include helping clients with vision and strategy development, people development and executive presence. And I was starting to feel confident that I had created my own unique way of coaching senior

---

*For practical exercises to build your own Personal Foundation, see the audio CD "Building Your Personal Foundation" at www.valwilliams.com

executives in these areas.

Then one day a more experienced, older consultant called and invited me to lunch. I was already impressed with this guy's track record and agreed with many of his philosophies around leadership. I was both surprised and very flattered when during our phone call, he proposed the idea of hiring me to present his seminars. He was so successful that he had more clients than he had capacity to deliver his training seminars.

When I arrived at the upscale Manhattan bistro and met him in person for the first time, he looked just as successful as he was: well dressed, sophisticated, clearly comfortable in this restaurant, and very self-possessed. After we ordered, he outlined more of his plans for collaborating. I was thrilled even to be considered. What an exciting deal! I would have a steady stream of work, be well compensated, and learn from a successful person whom I liked and respected. And the content of the work matched my general interests.

I left the meeting saying, "This is exciting, and I'll think about it." I didn't hide the fact that I was impressed by his knowledge and the potential of the position. It was a dream offer.

But something way in the back of my mind was hesitating. At first, I assumed it was just my normal fear of change. But the little feeling was saying in a small quiet voice: "No. This is a beautiful opportunity, but not right for you." I was really upset with myself. Here I thought I had developed clarity over the years on the type of work I liked, and this seemed to be it! What's the problem?

It took a few weeks for me to get greater clarity. And then, through conversations with my coach and my friends, I got it. There was an additional thing I had come to value over the years: my own voice, my own original ideas and my own approach to work.

It was true that for me to present this consultant's seminars would be good work, but it wouldn't be my work. It would be presenting someone else's ideas about leadership. And the small voice in the back of my head was now crystal clear: "It's time for you to present your own ideas about leadership — your views, your voice." Another part of me tried to argue: "But I'm not sure I can even summarize what my own ideas are." And my small voice said quietly, "Then it's time to begin. Stay in the question. What is your own view?"

And with that, I took a deep breath, called the consultant and turned down a lucrative and exciting deal. I lost that project, but I had gained real clarity. I needed to express my own perspective.

That's when I started writing this book.

The 3 Cs for Leaders

COURAGE *n.* the quality of mind or spirit that enables one to face danger or hardship with confidence and resolution; backbone

"You can do anything if you're willing to deal with the response. I'd take whatever anybody would dish out for the right to be myself."

— *WHOOPI GOLDBERG*

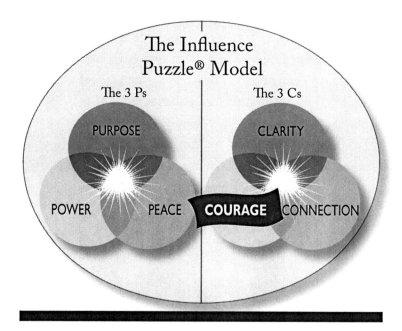

COURAGE

Demonstrate the Courage to move people forward in spite of their fears.

What Is Courage?

Leading at the top of the house is a tough game. Every senior leader is faced with situations that call for personal courage.

Courage helps you deal confidently with difficult or even threatening situations. Courage is making hard decisions when they are unpopular. Courage is speaking your mind even when your peers do not agree. Courage is saying "no" to things that you don't believe in, even when it's risky to do so. *Courage is taking risks and being able to face the consequences.*

To have strong influential presence, you need courage simply because you can't please all the people all the time. Leaders who have strong and creative vision have to sell their vision to people who do not share their views and opinions. Once you step up to a significant leadership position, to be a serious player, you need courage.

You may think that people who have courage do not have fear. But as a popular movie said, "It's not brave if you're not afraid." Courage is actually a decision to overcome your fear and take action anyway.

Benefits of Courage

When it comes to presence, courage is something people sense in a leader. They also recognize its absence in a leader. When the work ahead is scary or difficult, people need to know that they can trust and follow a leader. People have their own fears, so in order to go forward and overcome those fears, they need to be confident that the person leading them has the courage to keep going even when things get tough. If people sense a lack of courage in a leader's presence, they often will be tentative in their performance or not follow a leader at all.

Leaders with courage model a valuable way of being for others. *Courage is about being authentic, being your real, genuine self.* The intention of this ingredient of The Influence Puzzle® Model is to remind us to repeatedly ask ourselves: "Who do I want to be?"

Working in a large organization means that you are experiencing that organization's culture. Subtle organizational messages tell the leader all day long, "In this organization, we do things this way. In this organization, we value and reward these things. Therefore, in this organization, you need to be this type of leader." It can be easy to forget who you really are when steeped in a strong organizational culture. This can be especially true for high achievers, who are often experts at adapting to an organization's culture in the pursuit of success.

It takes courage to resist the organization's indoctrination.

It takes courage to be yourself, to find that delicate balance between supporting the team and contributing your unique and new viewpoint. But that is what the greatest leaders do.

Courage and Vulnerability

Courage and vulnerability have an interesting connection when it comes to leadership.

> The meaning of the word "vulnerable" is "exposed; open to attack; subject to criticism."
>
> The meaning of the word "courage" is "the state of mind enabling one to face danger or hardship with confidence and resolution."

Many people in leadership positions actually go to great lengths to avoid vulnerability. *In fact, many leaders have been trained to believe the incorrect notion that a leader's job is be invulnerable.*

> The meaning of the word invulnerable is "immune to attack; incapable of being damaged or injured; unable to be changed or criticized."

Successful leadership absolutely includes vulnerability. Leaders are all vulnerable. People are all vulnerable. We may resist that fact and try to pretend we are not. We like to hide behind invulnerable images. When we feel threatened, we often assume a tougher image. However, none of this posturing actually changes the fact that, as human beings, we are all vulnerable. Even the best leaders get criticized for new ideas.

Some leaders have to wait until history proves them to have been right long after they are gone. As leaders, we make real mistakes. Leaders get attacked just because they are in the leadership role. How many times have we suffered because "it happened on your watch"?

The Alpha Leader

So your ability to have courage also includes the ability to accept your own vulnerability instead of trying to defend against it. One of my specialties is coaching senior executives who are Alpha Males and Alpha Females (being a recovering Alpha myself). A large part of our work is looking at the several layers of armor that Alphas carry into every situation. At some point, that armor starts getting in the way, and *what was once viewed as youthful ambition and drive is later viewed as getting results but being too harsh with people.*

The turning point in coaching comes when the Alpha leader realizes that vulnerability is a fact, not a weakness. *Genuinely powerful people do not have to pretend that they are invulnerable by presenting an unapproachable, harsh front.* Truly powerful people do not have to be overly harsh with others to get results. Do genuinely powerful leaders hold people accountable? Yes. Are they often tough in confrontive situations? Yes. Are they firm in providing constructive feedback? Yes. But all this can be done without alienating people, without overreacting with anger, and without using criticism to strip other people of their self-esteem. Truly powerful people just don't behave that way. Insecure leaders behave that way.

To be effective, the Alpha leader must come to see that shedding layers of armor is actually a confirmation of strength and personal security. They must recognize that they are vulnerable, and that courage means feeling vulnerable and stepping forward anyway. This is where the other parts of The Influence Puzzle® Model are helpful. It is easier to be both vulnerable and courageous when you have developed a sense of inner peace, when you are clear about your purpose and when you realize the right use of your power.

This is another example of how all six ways of being: Purpose, Power, Peace and Clarity, Courage and Connection are much more powerful when a leader practices them simultaeously.

Courage Pays Off: Stuart

Leaders show courage in a variety of ways. Stuart is an Executive Vice President who leads a team of functional VPs in a telecommunications company. Each year the company requires Stuart and the other EVPs to have a formal, written 360-degree review. The 360 results are shared only with Stuart and the CEO he reports to. However, Stuart started a practice that surprised both his subordinates and his peers. For the past three years, Stuart has shared his unedited, written 360 results with all his direct reports. It is not a sanitized summary of feedback. He is showing the actual feedback comments that he received from his boss, peers and others. And due to recent marketing pressures and downsizings, the company culture is quite competitive, with the usual rough politics.

Stuart's direct reports admire his personal courage. Stuart also encourages them to give him more feedback, directly in real time, related to his own development goals. As a result of his willingness to be vulnerable people enjoy working for Stuart. His people are also very open with him on their own developmental needs. He models the fact that even excellent performers have areas to strengthen.

Naturally, when it comes to influencing his direct reports, Stuart is very influential. They trust him. They are willing to take risks in their own performance because they know that, although he will hold them accountable, he will also always look for the learning, even in mistakes. Stuart's courage directly impacts his staff's willingness to go for bigger results.

Assessing your own Courage

How do you know how fully you have developed your Courage? Here are some useful questions to ask yourself.

➤ How satisfied are you that you stand up for yourself?

➤ How well do you as a leader withstand criticism and disapproval?

➤ How well do you express your opinion, even in controversial situations?

➤ How comfortable are you at looking in the mirror at your own internal limitations, your own dark side?

➤ How clear are you on your criteria for walking away from a job, a relationship or a project?

➤ How comfortable are you giving difficult feedback on performance issues or on peer working relationship issues?

➤ How satisfied are you that you push back with superiors?

➤ How comfortable are you in being authentic, your real self?

➤ How well do you enforce your personal boundaries?

➤ How comfortable are you with taking risks?

➤ How willing are you to point out the elephant in the room?

My Own Journey to Courage

Again, I have to begin with a disclaimer: I do not yet have courage "handled." I'm working on it, and I have made some progress.

For me, courage has shown up in small ways and large ways. I have learned that courage is really personal. What takes a lot of courage for me to do may be easy for someone else to do. So I don't think courage can be judged by another person. Only you know.

Over the years, I have had many opportunities to demonstrate courage. Sometimes I rose to the occasion, and sometimes I did not. Sometimes I avoided the situation or took the easy way out. But one significant opportunity for courage that taught me a lot was quitting my corporate job to start my own business.

I had worked hard to become a corporate executive, and I really enjoyed corporate life. This sounds superficial, but in addition to the challenging work and the constant learning, I enjoyed every perk that corporate life offered: the big office, the travel, the title, leading a staff of hundreds of people, the big projects, the power. I enjoyed all of this and felt as if I had arrived. However, although I felt successful, something was missing. I wanted to feel more of the passion that I felt when I was working with people on their professional development, or when I was presenting ideas related to leadership.

Even after my experience of "being on fire" while presenting training seminars to my staff, I didn't see any way to incorporate that passion into the job I had. I was running a healthcare operation with heavy emphasis on production. I also didn't see any possibility of leaving my job. This career as a corporate executive is what I had strived so many years to achieve. But my nagging feeling of wanting to do more with developing people and learning with people ... that nagging feeling persisted.

Then I started getting clues from life. One of my internal company mentors who had heard me talk for years about my love for training people and this growing inner conflict finally said, "Val, you always talk about your true interests. You just need to leave the company and go do them." Slowly, the idea of actually leaving my job started to feel possible.

I was also taking various personal development classes—all confirming that people are happiest and most successful when they follow their passion. So, over time, and with a lot of help from mentors, teachers, classes, and a therapist, I gained clarity and came to the point of wanting to leave my corporate job and explore my true interests.

But I felt blocked by one thing: *fear of failure.*

What if I quit my great job and never really found what I was looking for? At night, I had scary, fearful images of ending up being a waitress at the same restaurant where all my high-powered colleagues and I usually had lunch. In my nightmares, my colleagues would be whispering about my failure and how stupid I was to quit my job.

I worked with one of my teachers who helped put my fears into perspective. At one point, when I insisted that "no matter what I decided to do, I had to be successful," she paused for a long moment and then said, "Of course. Be successful. But by whose standards?"

Hmmm. I wasn't sure of my answer to that question.

How much of my corporate climb had been to achieve success based on society's standards versus my own personal definitions of success?

Finally, it was a talk with my mother that was very significant for me. In a quiet moment during a family gathering at her house, she was sitting on her bed, flipping through a magazine, and I was sitting in the rocking chair at the foot of the bed — not too close, so she couldn't see how upset I was. Tentatively, I shared my career dilemma with her. I knew my mother was proud of my corporate success so I was very careful in my presentation, not wanting her to feel disappointed that I was considering such a huge change: leaving my job.

But my mother's response was hugely supportive and really surprised me. She said, "Val, your whole life you were a good kid, and you pretty much did everything we wanted you to do. But you've never done just what you want to do."

That wasn't what I expected to hear so it brought me to tears. And then I dared to speak my real fear.

"But Mom," I said, looking down, embarrassed to show that I was crying. "What if I don't make it; what if I fail?" Just saying that out loud upset me even more.

My mom did not appear upset at all. She answered right away, "What if you don't make it? We'll still love you."

I relaxed a lot after that.

Soon after, I was sitting in front of my boss — in my wonderful corporate office that I had worked so hard to attain — saying the one sentence that I knew would change my life: "I've decided to resign."

I was still afraid, but I was free.

The 3 Cs for Leaders

CONNECTION *n.* the act of joining; alliance; a bond, a link; anything that joins, relates or connects

> *"When we seek for connection, we restore the world to wholeness. Our seemingly separate lives become meaningful as we discover how truly necessary we are to each other."*
>
> — *MARGARET WHEATLEY*

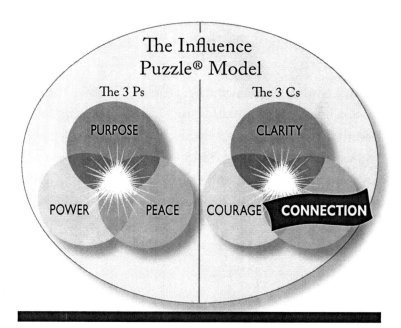

CONNECTION

Build the Connections that invite people to trust you.

What Is Connection?

Think of the leaders you admire. You probably have some sense of connection. When people are emotionally invested and connected to a leader, they also tend to feel a sense of pride and satisfaction in being a part of the leader's vision. Connection with people is the backbone of presence because, although it is more difficult to describe in actual behavioral terms, it's what people really feel from a leader.

Connection is experienced by people through a leader's speech, body language and, for lack of a better term, general vibration. Connection is the intangible sense that lets people know intuitively whether a leader is approachable or not. The degree of connection also tells people how helpful the leader will be, how close people can get to him/her, and how much they can build a trusting relationship with the leader.

This intangible feeling that people perceive comes from inside a leader who values connection. True connection is based on empathy, understanding and caring about people, particularly the people you lead — direct reports and colleagues. Connection can be seen when leaders cultivate a friendly interest in people. Ease of connecting comes from a basic mindset of respect for people, an understanding that people are usually doing the best they can with what they know at the time, and a basic belief that everybody's worthy and, given time and opportunity, everybody is interesting.

Connection is a major part of a leader's job since strong leaders are connected to their followers, to their peers, to the people they work for, to their customers, and to the industry and world at large. *A major part of leadership is working these connections.* So connection means a leader needs to be comfortable forming alliances at all levels: the individual level, the team level and the system level. It is through these connections that a leader gets things done.

Some people confuse connection with friendship. Leaders sometimes think that to be connected to others is to be in a full friendship with others. However, connection is not the same as friendship. Connection only requires that you build a bridge with another person, and that you're able to exchange ideas and feelings with another person, that you're able to impact another person. *Leaders need to be in connection with large numbers of people. However, leaders do not need to be friends with all those people.* It's important to clarify this because leaders often shy away from connection because they are concerned that a lot of connection means an overwhelming amount of relationship with other people. And that's not the case. Other leaders may get into trouble or decrease their influence because they go past connection into friendship, or they confuse connection with friendship.

Connection and Influence

So what's the relationship between being able to connect with people in a peaceful, trusting way and being influential? Many leaders think they are effective at influencing people's behavior through the authority of their position or by using fear to push people into action. But when you need people to change their behavior or move into action, you will have greater long-term success if people experience you as encouraging rather than intimidating. People are generally anxious about change. They are much more likely to move forward and even be excited about the change if your presence balances courage and determination to make changes with the ability to connect to real people.

Of course there are times when a leader has to be firm, even confrontational. The distinction is this: Is the leader being firm or tough deliberately as a strategy to handle a specific leadership situation? *Or, as is often the case, is the leader being overly harsh simply out of frustration and inability to get the results they want?* The difference between these two ways of being is significant.

Intimidation can get people moving. In the short run human beings can be made to fear a leader and then take action out of that fear. However, leadership by intimidation is not a sustainable strategy for success with people over time. That way of leading is similar to eating sugary junk food: you get an initial short burst of energy, and then later you get a crash and fatigue.

Lack of Engagement

While some leaders don't connect with people because they choose to intimidate, others don't connect because of apathy, fear, or not making the time. Many leaders are unengaged with their people because they feel they are too busy with what they consider the real work.

Today's firefighting may often take precedence over having regularly scheduled one-on-one meetings with direct reports. Some leaders are just not comfortable connecting with people beyond strictly work subjects like status updates on projects. Some leaders hide out in their office, believing they are too tied up with emails to walk around talking to people. And many leaders just do not realize how critical it is to leadership success to connect with their people. In some cases, a leader may not understand that connections are a foundation for getting the work done.

Benefits of Connection

When you connect with people in a way that is peaceful, supportive and without conflict, people want to follow you as a leader. With this level of connection, you then have the rapport to seriously challenge people to perform at their best. So this is not about backing off from getting measurable business results. Authentic connection enhances business results.

Connection enables you to motivate people to go further, to disagree respectfully, and to manage conflict well. As a result

ple are inspired. When you create connection, people
ant to work with you and support your purpose. When
you have relationships that are not peaceful, when they are
based on conflict, criticism or fear, then people may obey
your authority as a leader, but they do not see you as inspiring
or powerful and ultimately will not follow.

Connecting Well: Lynn

Lynn is Chief Operating Officer of a major financial
services company. People admire Lynn because in spite of
her C-level job, she goes out of her way to create time
for relationship and connection. Inside the company she
surprised people by being a participant of the internal
mentoring program where she personally mentors one
assigned mentee each year. She also is a speaker at the
company's annual career conference and actually stays for
the cocktail and networking hour that evening.

Outside of work she plans her very busy travel
schedule to accommodate combining seeing customers
with visiting at least one friend whenever she can. Most
importantly, people describe Lynn as "very approachable
for a COO!" As one of her direct reports said, "When
I deal with Lynn, there is nothing in the way; nothing
between her and me. I can feel the real person there,
not just the senior executive."

This level of connection has earned Lynn a good deal
of loyalty from colleagues. Lynn has worked in three
different companies over her career and she has brought
colleagues with her each time. Her connections have
helped her build strong leadership teams that work well

together, so she has been able to produce strong results in all three companies. For Lynn, connection is not just a nice idea. It is a business strategy.

The Most Important Connection

Successful leaders need to develop strong connections with others to build followership. *However, the most important connection that you as a leader must have is the connection to yourself.* As outlined in the Introduction, it is very easy to lose your way in the corporate maze.

I often remind senior executives to take time off alone to recharge, rest and, most important, to get back in touch with themselves. In addition to other executive development activities, leaders should also be working on their personal development. Otherwise there is the danger of becoming rather one-dimensional, where life is composed of work—work social events, work friends, and not much else.

One simple way of continually exploring who you are and connecting with yourself is cultivating hobbies, leisure activities and friends outside your industry. Challenge yourself by trying activities at which you are not very skilled.

One of the best assignments my own coach gave me was to take action on something I had always been interested in, but felt I had no time to do. So I started pottery classes. My coach also gave me one key instruction: I was not allowed to discuss my work or what I did for a living at the pottery class. I was there to learn, connect with other students and connect with my own experience.

I found this tremendously challenging. The first thing that I noticed is how quiet I was in the class because once I couldn't talk about work, I realized that I did not have much else to say. I felt pretty insecure. And on top of that, I was not good at pottery. My pottery wheel was completely out of control. I was wearing more clay on my clothes than I had on the wheel. I had even selected the wrong clothes for class. (I thought a brand new white one piece overall was quite fashionable. Let's just say that was a poor choice...).

However, over 10 weeks, I did manage to produce several oddly shaped, unattractive but functional, shiny blue bowls. All of our work was eligible for sale in the gift shop, but none of my work was chosen. In spite of this lack of achievement on my part, the biggest surprise of all was that I had fun.

I learned about myself— that I don't have to be the leader all the time. I learned that I can survive embarrassment. I saw how critical I initially can be of my own creations. I experienced my own shyness at meeting new people when I can't hide behind my professional role. And I saw something I really liked about myself. In the end, I was able to feel real love for my unattractive odd bowls, just because I had made them. I experienced feeling connected with me regardless of my ability to achieve the goal. I probably failed as a potter, but I enjoyed a new aspect of myself.

Assessing your own Connection

How do you know how fully you have developed the quality of Connection? Here are some useful questions to ask yourself.

➤ How satisfied are you with the depth of relationship you have with peers, subordinates, bosses, customers and industry colleagues?

➤ How would others judge your ability to have them feel connected to you?

➤ How well do you make people right versus make people wrong?

➤ Are you accelerating connection by building rapport vs. assuming "it takes time"?

➤ How satisfied are you that you have enough strategic alliances with the right people?

➤ Do you have enough intimate connections with people who will tell you the unvarnished truth?

➤ How comfortable are you with being vulnerable, even in work relationships?

➤ How connected are you to your own feelings?

➤ How connected are you with your real source of power, which is your connection with yourself?

My Own Journey to Connection

For many people, connection is easy, and even natural. For me, connection has been the most intimidating ingredient of the six parts of The Influence Puzzle® model. People who know me have been surprised by this because it appears contradictory. When it comes to my clients, I have always connected exceptionally well and have deeply enjoyed those connections. As long as I was in the arena of work, connecting just wasn't a problem.

However, it became clear to me that the reason connections with clients and co-workers on a project were easy for me was because we all knew what to expect. Everyone had a clearly defined role. For example: "I am the coach or consultant. You are the client that I serve." We were usually focused on a particular task and we all knew the general direction of things.

But in personal friendships, I struggled with connection. In friendships, the roles are not clear. Who does what and when? There are many more emotions involved. What is OK to feel? What does my friend expect of me? Is it OK to expect something of my friend? Do we just follow our intuition? Or is there a right way to be friends? What if I can't fulfill the other person's expectations? We are both busy; how will we find time for the friendship?

These were the types of questions I had but felt too embarrassed to ask anyone. They sounded like stupid questions that I should have mastered in high school. I feared that if I talked about these concerns, someone would say: "How old are you? Twelve?" So in the area of personal relationships, I basically stayed introverted and fairly guarded.

Luckily for me, I met several very cool people who wanted to be friends with me and looked beyond my protective barrier. Over time I made it a specific goal for myself to create an inner circle of at least five close friends. I am blessed to have those friends today. Having these close connections has also taught me things about life that I might never have learned on my own. Close friends tell you the truth about your own blind spots. Then you can grow in some unexpected ways.

For example, there was a woman I had known casually as a colleague for several years. We went to the same conferences and knew many of the same people. Through a series of unplanned events, we ended up spending lots of time together and happily became real friends. When I told her I was working on strengthening my own ability for connection, she asked if I wanted feedback, which I accepted.

She said, "Val, even though I knew you for many years, and we were always pleasant, I never felt that I could really connect with you. I always felt you had this force field up that kept people at a distance." I was stunned to hear this—not just the content, but also her candor. She went on: "It was like you were clear that nobody was going to get beyond your force field without your permission, so it put me off."

And then, just when I was trying to decide if I should be defensive or grateful, she added: "And the reason I can see this so clearly in you is because I used to have the same kind of force field with people myself."

I relaxed and she went on to share a perspective I

found really helpful. She said: "I totally understand the protection a force field provides, and I'm not suggesting you get rid of it. But instead of your barrier being like 25 feet outside of your body, bring the force field inside you. That way you can allow people in much closer to you. But if for whatever reason you discover that someone is not a match for you, you can still have your boundaries." That satisfied both my cautious nature and my need to break out of my old way of being.

So I have practiced connection with these new learnings. And amazingly, all my connections have improved. I always knew that connection was a critical part of being an influential presence. I thought the lessons for a leader were obvious — have great connections with the people you lead and with peers, colleagues, family and friends. But I did not realize how many subtle layers there can be to this whole topic of connection. Even people who appear on the surface to have good connections can often go much deeper and broader.

I continue to work on strengthening my ability to connect. I have a feeling that even the progress I have made so far is only the beginning.

Living The Influence Puzzle® Model

"There is a big difference between knowing the path and walking the path."

— FROM THE MOTION PICTURE "THE MATRIX"

SUMMARY
The Influence Puzzle® Model

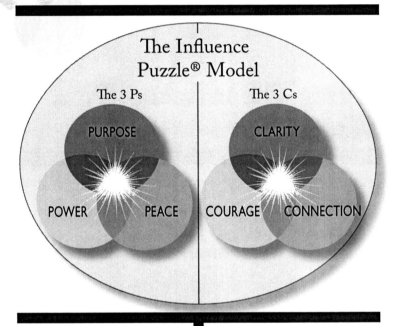

The Influence
Puzzle® Model

The 3 Ps

The 3 Cs

PURPOSE

CLARITY

POWER   PEACE

COURAGE   CONNECTION

The 3 Ps

Purpose
Declare the Purpose that
prompted you to step up
to lead.

Power
Demonstrate the right use
of your Power

Peace
Find the Peace that creates
conditions for creativity
and innovation

The 3 Cs

Clarity
Create the Clarity that
inspires people to follow.

Courage
Demonstrate the Courage
to move people forward in
spite of their fears.

Connection
Build the Connections
that invite people to trust
you.

Living The Influence Puzzle® Model

The Influence Puzzle® Model is meant to be more than a philosophical idea. As a leader, we have to live the model to experience its benefits. That means demonstrating all six components to the best of our ability on a daily basis. These are the six reminders for a leader's presence, six questions to ask yourself to guide your daily actions. At the end of today, ask yourself the following questions. Reflect on examples that support your personal assessment.

The 6 Influence Puzzle Coaching Questions

1. How well did I live my **Purpose** today?

2. What did I do today to demonstrate the right use of my **Power**?

3. How well did I maintain my inner **Peace**?

4. How did I demonstrate **Clarity**?

5. Where did I show **Courage**?

6. How well did I achieve **Connection**?

Presence may seem like an indefinable quality but it can be both identified and strengthened. *The six major ingredients of presence: Purpose, Power, Peace, Clarity, Courage, Connection are at the root of almost every challenge a*

leader faces. So one of these best ways to be more effective as a senior executive leader is to consciously develop your presence.

Intellectual knowing—just reading this book and understanding what you read—is not the same thing as putting the model into your life as a ***practice***. When a leader actually lives The Influence Puzzle® Model, people experience truly influential and beneficial leadership.

The Influence Puzzle® for Organizations

The Influence Puzzle® Model can be applied on many levels. The Influence Puzzle® helps you as an executive to lead more effectively, and these same principles also help you in your personal life. You can look at the six parts of the model for your role as a parent, as a volunteer, as a friend.

The Influence Puzzle® Model is also effective as a leadership paradigm in organizations. ***Although many organizations have leadership competency lists, very few have guidance and tools for leadership presence.*** The six-part Influence Puzzle Model is applicable for leaders who aspire to move into senior leadership. The model is especially useful for those high achievers who are newly promoted or about to make the transition to Vice President or C-level roles.

The Influence Puzzle® Model is especially powerful when applied to both individual senior executive leaders and teams of leaders. ***Therefore, an organization can build*** *an entire culture of strong leadership in which every one of its leaders has a powerful influential presence. Here's how:*

As an individual senior executive is coached to start living the six ingredients of The Influence Puzzle® Model, their team of direct reports are coached on the model. When I coach a team of leaders together to develop their influence through their presence, the team also experiences a wonderful team-building effect by learning together.

For example, I coached a group of leaders of an employee benefits company and the participants had an experience that helped to strengthen their team. In this Influence Puzzle seminar, the team coaching exercises were highly interactive as the leaders worked through the six parts of the model. These leaders shared their individual purposes with each other. Each leader came out of their "silo" to share their challenges around connecting with customers. The leaders supported each other in having the courage to withstand the pressure associated with the tough decisions they had to make on pricing. The whole team helped each other deepen their knowledge of how to put together The Influence Puzzle®, while incorporating their own views on what it really takes to influence in their specific company. As a result, the whole leadership team became more influential.

The Possibilities for Organizations

So what's possible if an entire organization becomes more influential? Imagine the power and impact of an organization that influences customers more effectively, influences the marketplace and influences how its industry evolves.

Think of The Influence Puzzle® Model's ingredients: Purpose, Power, Peace, Clarity, Courage and Connection. Imagine an entire organization where every leader, every individual contributor, every vendor to the company is crystal clear on the company's purpose. What if every executive, every supervisor, and every technician demonstrated the courage to take risks while balancing that courage with knowing the right use of their power? What if everyone in the organization valued connection: connection to peers, staff, customers, industry colleagues? And what if every leader, every technician, could do all this in a balanced way — understanding how to balance the power to get results with the inner peace required for long-term sustainability?

An organization that did all of this would be living a culture of influence and presence, demonstrating all six aspects of the model. What type of impact would be possible for this type of organization? What could such an organization achieve for its customers? What kind of productivity would we see from employees in an organization where the senior executive leaders were all viewed as role models of The Influence Puzzle® Model? This would mean that employees and customers would look at these senior executives as leaders who have solved the puzzle of how to influence. These leaders would be seen as:

- ➤ purposeful
- ➤ skilled at using power well
- ➤ strong and peaceful
- ➤ crystal clear in how they communicate
- ➤ courageous
- ➤ easy to connect with

How would the bottom line be affected? How would these types of leaders view profit? Expenses? Strategic planning? How would leaders who live The Influence Puzzle® Model view people development? Delegation? Execution? What type of work environment would they create? What type of large-scale initiatives would they create?

With an appreciation for both profit and purpose, imagine what is possible for leaders and organizations that have developed this type of powerful influential presence.

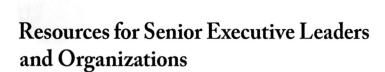

Resources for Senior Executive Leaders and Organizations

If this book has resonated with you, then we believe you will enjoy learning to strengthen your influential presence. Contact us to participate in one of our many programs.

The Influence Puzzle® programs are available in flexible formats for organizations:

- ➤ The Influence Puzzle® Individual Executive Coaching Programs

- ➤ The Influence Puzzle® Retreats for Leadership Teams

- ➤ The Influence Puzzle® Seminars for Groups of Leaders

To bring any of The Influence Puzzle® Programs to your organization, or to find an Executive Coach who has been specifically trained in coaching senior executives on The Influence Puzzle® Model, contact us:

Val Williams

www.valwilliams.com

val@valwilliams.com

732-632-9647

Acknowledgements

I am grateful to many people who helped me create this book.

> ◇ Thank you to every one of my clients for giving me the privilege of coaching you and learning deeper lessons about leadership with you.

> ◇ Thank you to my own coach and my teachers for supporting me and coaching me to better articulate my message.

> ◇ Thank you to my close friends who encouraged me in spite of my protests to write more candidly about my own experience.

> ◇ Thank you to my husband, Randy Holmes, for the question that first sparked the idea for this book: "Isn't the central theme of all of your work executive presence?"

About Val Williams

Val Williams, MCC, is an Executive Development Consultant and Leadership Expert who has coached and consulted with hundreds of senior corporate executives and their teams in companies around the globe since 1994.

Val specializes in helping senior corporate leaders develop and strengthen the critical senior leadership capabilities: influence, vision development, strategic planning, team alignment, execution and people development. She provides consulting services, training seminars, team coaching, keynotes and management retreats to the organization-at-large, as well as individual executive coaching services.

Val's past experience as a corporate executive herself has included leading organizations of over 700 people in multiple locations in the Managed Healthcare industry at Prudential, managing an operating budget of $25 million. Val is a graduate of Tufts University with a Bachelor of Science and a graduate of Boston University with a Master's Degree in Counseling Psychology. A frequent and dynamic speaker at corporate management retreats and industry functions, Val is credentialed as a Master Certified Coach by the International Coach Federation, and has authored several books including *Get the Best Out of Your People and*

Yourself, Virtual Leadership, Executive Think Time, Executive Foundation, and *Butterfly Coaching.*

For more information on how working with Val Williams can help you, your team and your organization develop the leadership skills that can take you to the top of your field, visit Val's website at: **www.valwilliams.com** or call 732.632.9647.

Share It With Others

If you'd like to order more books, complete this form and fax it to us (877) 443-4092, or visit our website to email us and see other products: www.valwilliams.com

QTY	Product	Price	Total
	The Influence Puzzle®	$14.95	
	Sales Tax: (NJ residents add 7%)		
	Shipping/Handling (Add $2.00)		
		Total	

Shipping Address

Name			
Address 1			
Address 2			
City	State	Zip/Postal Code	Country
Phone		Fax	
Email			

Charge To:

Cardholder Name

Credit Card Number(Circle One):   Visa   Master Card   American Express

Expiration Date (MM/YY)

If paying by check, mail check and completed form to:
Shadowbrook Publishing
P.O. Box 2458
Edison, New Jersey 08818
Checks payable to Shadowbrook Publishing

TO ORDER
Visit our website: **www.valwilliams.com**
Or Fax 877-443-4092
Our books are also available on Amazon.com

Other Books and Recordings
by Val Williams

Get the Best Out of Your People and Yourself:
7 Practical Steps for Top Performance

This book gives 7 practical steps for leaders and executives who want to see top performance from the staff. The handbook gives excellent practical instructions on delegation, giving feedback, performance management, and coaching your people.

(100 pages. $14.95 + $2 shipping)

Virtual Leadership

This little booklet gives leaders lots of tips for how to manage and coach their people when the staff is located in a different city or different country. When staff is in a different geographic location, how do you evaluate performance? Coach performance? Build a team? Have successful teleconferences? This booklet gives solutions.

(40 pages. $6.95 + $1.50 shipping)

Building Your Personal Foundation:
7 Steps for a Happier Life (Audio CD)

Building your Personal Foundation will show you how to:
- Raise your standards
- Get your needs met
- Eliminate what you tolerate
- Restore integrity
- Build boundaries
  and more!

($10 + $1 shipping)

Executive Think Time: Thinking That Gets Results

Most leaders are so busy, they don't take enough time to think. Ellen Fredericks and Val Williams wrote the book, *Executive Think Time: Thinking That Gets Results.* This book gives leaders a simple, 4-step model to take their thinking to a higher level. A great solution for leaders who want to be less reactive and create results.

(105 pages. $14.95 + $2 shipping)

Executive Think Time Training Seminars

Val Williams presents on-site training seminars to roll out the 4-step Executive Think Time model to entire management teams. Seminars are customized to the organization's needs.

Contact Val for details. www.valwilliams.com

Executive Foundation

This book is designed for new, seasoned, or aspiring executives to assess and improve the strength of their Executive Foundation, the essential skills that make a successful senior leader. Val Williams and Ellen Fredericks ask: "How satisfied are you with your own Executive Foundation?" Take the Executive Foundation Assessment and find out!

(62 pages. $12.95 + $2 shipping)

Executive Foundation Coaching Programs

The assessment in the book, Executive Foundation, shows executives both their strengths and areas for improvement in executive skills. Executive Foundation coaching programs are designed for individuals and/or teams to strengthen their leadership skills, based on this assessment.

Leadership: Three Essential Questions for Executives

(Audio CD)

This audio CD is a conversation between Val Williams and Joan Wright, focusing on the future of executive coaching and leadership, and the three most critical factors that leaders need to address to ensure success.

($14.95 + $1 shipping)

Butterfly Coaching

Developing people is the key to a successful organization and achieving results. So why is it so difficult to help people develop and evolve? This book offers a three-step model and tool for effectively developing people and creating lasting individual and organizational change. You'll discover why the usual methods of advising and helping don't work, as well as more effective alternatives.

($6.95 + $2 shipping)

CPSIA information can be obtained at www.ICGtesting.com
Printed in the USA
BVOW04s1515310713

327415BV00004B/11/P